Cambridge Elements ≡

Elements in Critical Issues in Teacher Education
edited by
Tony Loughland
University of New South Wales
Andy Gao
University of New South Wales
Hoa T. M. Nguyen
University of New South Wales

ENHANCING EDUCATORS' THEORETICAL AND PRACTICAL UNDERSTANDINGS OF CRITICAL LITERACY

Vera Sotirovska

Margaret Vaughn
Washington State University

CAMBRIDGE
UNIVERSITY PRESS

Shaftesbury Road, Cambridge CB2 8EA, United Kingdom

One Liberty Plaza, 20th Floor, New York, NY 10006, USA

477 Williamstown Road, Port Melbourne, VIC 3207, Australia

314–321, 3rd Floor, Plot 3, Splendor Forum, Jasola District Centre,
New Delhi – 110025, India

103 Penang Road, #05–06/07, Visioncrest Commercial, Singapore 238467

Cambridge University Press is part of Cambridge University Press & Assessment,
a department of the University of Cambridge.

We share the University's mission to contribute to society through the pursuit of
education, learning and research at the highest international levels of excellence.

www.cambridge.org
Information on this title: www.cambridge.org/9781009304702

DOI: 10.1017/9781009304726

© Vera Sotirovska and Margaret Vaughn 2023

This publication is in copyright. Subject to statutory exception and to the provisions
of relevant collective licensing agreements, no reproduction of any part may take
place without the written permission of Cambridge University Press & Assessment.

First published 2023

A catalogue record for this publication is available from the British Library

ISBN 978-1-009-30470-2 Paperback
ISSN 2755-1202 (online)
ISSN 2755-1199 (print)

Cambridge University Press & Assessment has no responsibility for the persistence
or accuracy of URLs for external or third-party internet websites referred to in this
publication and does not guarantee that any content on such websites is, or will
remain, accurate or appropriate.

Enhancing Educators' Theoretical and Practical Understandings of Critical Literacy

Elements in Critical Issues in Teacher Education

DOI: 10.1017/9781009304726
First published online: August 2023

Vera Sotirovska

Margaret Vaughn
Washington State University

Author for correspondence: Vera Sotirovska, vera.sot88@gmail.com

Abstract: This Element explores ways to promote critical literacy in teacher education. First, the authors define critical literacy in the context of teacher education through established theoretical frameworks and models of critical literacy pedagogy and share their collective findings on critical literacy research over the course of a decade. Building from these theoretical understandings of critical literacy, they outline ways to actualize critical literacy in teacher education as a transformative pedagogy coupled with resources and activities that support equitable teaching practices. Next, they illustrate how adaptive teaching supports critical literacy pedagogy and underscore autoethnography as a reflective tool to engage pre-service teachers in critical literacy practice. They model this approach with mentor text analyses using critical literacy as a lens to facilitate critically oriented mindsets in teachers through visioning. They conclude with implications for classroom practice at the intersections of critical literacy and teacher preparation and provide directions for future research.

Keywords: critical literacy, teacher education, literacy methods, children's and young adult literature, critical literacy pedagogy

ISBNs: 9781009304702 (PB), 9781009304726 (OC)
ISSNs: 2755-1202 (online), 2755-1199 (print)

Contents

1 Introduction

Based on our collective research on critical literacy and teacher preparation over the last decade (Guerrettaz et al., 2022; Sotirovska & Kelley, 2020; Sotirovska & Vaughn, 2022ab, 2023; Vaughn, 2015; Vaughn & Kuby, 2019), in this Element, we contribute with theoretical and pedagogical approaches to advance teacher education practices to develop critically oriented teacher candidates. This Element is organized into ten sections. We start this discussion with a popular classroom text, *Skippyjon Jones* (Schachner, 2007), and highlight the importance of critical literacy in preparing pre-service teachers for today's classroom realities as the school-going population is becoming increasingly more diverse (see Section 2). To do this, we define critical literacy in the context of teacher education (see Section 3), discuss our key findings from multiple studies on critical literacy we conducted over the last several years (see Section 4), and emphasize the importance of reflective practice (see Sections 5 and 6), visioning (see Section 7), and autoethnographic methods (see Section 8) in developing critically minded educators. We also present supporting resources in the form of guiding questions for curriculum adaptations (Tables 4 and 5), case study examples from our teaching experiences (Sections 6 and 9), prompts for teacher reflection (Section 9), and an extensive list of children's and young adult literature to support critical literacy practices in teacher education and K-12 classrooms (see Appendix).

From our collective research in critical literacy, we introduce a critical literacy framework and eleven Critical Literacy Beliefs Survey (CLBS) actionable tenets that teacher educators can implement in their courses. Further, we list activities, strategies, and children's and young adult literature examples (see Section 9) that underscore these practices. We also discuss key concepts of critical literacy based on the four Lewison et al.'s (2002) critical literacy dimensions (disrupting the commonplace, interrogating multiple viewpoints, focusing on sociopolitical issues, and taking action and promoting social justice) and further engage with each dimension by adding questions for text analysis. Specifically, we share findings from our research study where we explored critical literacy as a construct and piloted a survey instrument (CLBS) modeled on Lewison et al.'s (2002) critical literacy framework. Moreover, we reflect on findings from a qualitative study about pre-service teachers' critical literacy beliefs to examine how the critical literacy framework (Lewison et al., 2002), can be operationalized through survey items representative of each dimension. These items were tested with a sample of pre-service teachers ($N = 405$) and eleven tenets of critical literacy were deduced for teacher education practice. Based on these findings, we illustrate how these tenets can be actualized with children's literature through classroom examples. We also present case studies from our critical literacy research that bridge critical literacy theory with teaching practice to support ways for teacher educators to implement reading supports that are equitable, responsive, and representative of students' experiences with schooling. Building from the survey findings, pre-service teacher interviews, and critical literacy framework (Lewison et al., 2002), we outline the role of adaptability in cultivating a critically oriented mindset in teacher candidates with deliberate attention to pedagogical practices. This section explores different modes of research such as autoethnography and visioning as valuable tools in working to orient and foster critically minded teacher candidates within teacher education programs. To conclude (see Section 10), we comment on materials and resources that can be used to engage teacher candidates with critical concepts.

2 Supporting Critical Literacy Practices through Children's Literature: Examples from Teacher Education Classrooms

During a recent observation, Mandy (pseudonym), a White, European American graduate student who had previously taught for nearly a decade as a public school teacher, began her read aloud of *Skippyjon Jones* (Schachner, 2007) during a writing methods course in a teacher preparation program at a public, land grant university in the Pacific Northwest region of the United States. The picture book, which hosts the main character, Skippyjon, a Siamese cat who thinks he is a Chihuahua, and who speaks mock Spanish, presents numerous stereotypes of Latinx peoples (Martínez-Roldán, 2013). With the exaggerated anthropomorphic characters that mimic the sound of the Spanish language through stereotypical representations (Martínez-Roldán, 2016), such texts depict misrepresentations of the Latinx culture, language, and ways of being (Rodríguez et al., 2021).

One student who described themself as being Mexican American explained "I feel like that book is making fun of me" (Senta, 2014, p. 55). However, this series was espoused as a model text during the teacher preparation writing methods class. As Janks (2000, 2010) has explicitly argued, language choice matters in how learners construct their identities; using mock narratives that perpetuate stereotypes exacerbates efforts to cultivate socially just and equitable learning environments. With the advance of many culturally relevant and engaging children's literature texts available (Campagnaro et al., 2021; Kelly et al., 2021), we wondered why such texts and practices inadvertently find their way into so many teacher preparation programs and what could be done to better support the development of critically oriented teacher candidates.

Unfortunately, we see many of these practices across the literature and in our research with teachers in schools, especially concerning the children's literature teachers use to teach literacy. For example, in two critical content analyses of children's literature depicting diversities (Gultekin & May, 2020; Rodríguez et al., 2021), researchers found that children's literature holds the potential to both perpetuate and challenge stereotypes of unrepresented children. As Gultekin and May (2020) argue that even award-winning books from established authors may convey outdated and inaccurate perspectives on historically underrepresented groups, which can magnify and/or minimize stereotypes and tropes about them. In their research, Gultekin and May (2020) found that Middle Eastern Muslim depictions in children's literature portrayed predominantly displaced protagonists from underdeveloped rural areas, which may lead to overgeneralization and stereotyping of the people from the Middle East without the complexities, geographical nuances, and diversities of their lived experiences. For example, the authors point out that one such example is *Mirror* (Baker, 2010) where two families are being compared, one in Valley of the Roses, Morocco and another one in Sydney, Australia. Gultekin and May (2020) find this text problematic because it compares two distinct lifestyles of the family living in the rural village of Valley of Roses, depicted tending to livestock, riding a donkey, and cooking in a clay oven, to that of a family living in a large metropolitan city, depicted working on a laptop, using modern kitchen appliances, and driving cars. The researchers explain that more adequate comparisons could have been made if the author had chosen "Morocco's Casablanca, with its metropolitan area population of 6.9 million … [as] a more suitable location to compare with Sydney, Australia" (Gultekin & May, 2020, p. 632). Like this, Dahlen (2021) argues that representation is not the ultimate goal of inclusive children's literature, but it is the accuracy, authenticity, and diversity in the portrayal of cultures, identities, and geographies across human histories. Hence, reading globally (Short, 2019) without a critical lens may limit readers' understandings and perpetuate monolithic views of these human diversities.

Though efforts have been made to stop the printing of books that convey reductionist stereotypes, many teachers still consider these books as strong examples of children's literature (Pratt, 2021). For example, Nel (2014) and Ishizuka (2019) explored how popular Dr. Seuss titles and adjacent works (comics, caricatures, and other illustrated works) contribute to harmful stereotyping of underrepresented groups. For example, the popular picture books, *And to Think That I Saw It on Mulberry Street* (Seuss, 1937) and *If I Ran the Zoo* (Seuss, 1950) are replete with tokenisms and exaggerated racial characteristics (Ishizuka, 2019). These tokens, for example, feature a racialized interpretation of East Asian and Middle Eastern characteristics, such as that of a man's turban in *If I Ran the Zoo*, which is caricatured by a White protagonist who bemuses about putting the man wearing a turban in a zoo. The depictions of Indigenous Native Americans in *Little House on the Prairie* (Wilder, 1935) have been criticized for the negative and reductionist portrayals (Smulders, 2002), a harmful phenomenon prevalent in other more recently published books, such as *The Indian in the Cupboard* (Banks, 2010), where an Indigenous Native American toy character is referred to as the "Indian" and *Alvin Ho* (Look, 2010), where Indigenous cultural emblems are misappropriated and presented as a Halloween costume rather than a traditional garb.

Given these portrayals, critical scholars emphasize the need for culturally accurate and authentic narratives as a pathway for readers to understand themselves, others, and the world (Bishop, 1990). Specifically, with the focus on accountability, student activism, and culturally responsive curricula, pre-service teachers are of a particular demographic that has been called to address ways to support equitable representation and practices in schooling through children's literature (Short, 2019). Ghiso et al. (2013) remind us that "Supporting our university students to better understand, learn from, and advocate for the multiple literacies of their students calls for a different orientation to 'accountability'" (p. 52). Fostering these critical orientations in pre-service teachers requires a step-by-step approach beginning in teacher preparation. For example, Lee (2020) shared *Visiting Day* (Woodson, 2002) with a group of pre-service teachers, which is a picture book about how a young girl and her grandmother prepare to visit the girl's father in prison. Lee applied Lewison et al.'s (2002) four dimensions of critical literacy as a lens through which pre-service teachers analyzed *Visiting Day* to understand how each dimension added a new layer of meaning to the book connecting it to larger social contexts, such as raising awareness of the varying family and school realities of children. After, to bridge the teacher preparation classroom with pre-service teachers' praxis, the pre-service teachers read *Maddi's Fridge* (Brandt & Vogel, 2014), a picture book about the disparaging socioeconomic realities of two best friends Sofia and Maddi with a group of elementary fourth grade students. The pre-service teachers applied the same critical literacy framework to engage the students in critical discussions about poverty. This study shows how pre-service teachers can develop a repertoire of reading supports that are equitable, responsive, and representative of students' lived experiences with schooling and their home realities. In this way, pre-service teachers can be taught critical literacy skills in the teacher preparation class-room using children's literature and then practice these skills in authentic classroom contexts.

A similar pathway toward supporting pre-service teachers is through literacy artifacts (i.e., picture books, textbooks, articles, etc.) underlined by critical literacy approaches, such as examining classroom artifacts from multiple perspectives (Fisher & Ivey, 2006). Literacy artifacts include, for example, picture books, textbooks, articles, images, videos, and other resources that act as a catalyst for analyzing tropes, dominant discourses, and master narratives (Kim & Short, 2019). Dominant discourses refer to how language is codified to express ideology, sociopolitical beliefs, biases, and worldviews often of a given social group (such as those of teachers) (Gee, 1990). Master narratives are dominant texts that may perpetuate hegemonic and one-sided perspectives of social phenomena (Lewison et al., 2015). Hence, pre-service teachers may actively learn to counter master narratives by inviting other viewpoints to gain a robust and more egalitarian understanding of the curricula being taught at schools (Botelho & Rudman, 2009). For instance, in Rodríguez et al. (2021), the key component in using children's literature as a transformative tool in teacher preparation was to train pre-service teachers to read children's literature through a critical lens that will develop critically oriented perspectives. In this research, pre-service teachers took part in a course centering on bilingualism, bilingual education, and Latinx youth in a Midwestern teacher preparation program. In this course, pre-service teachers analyzed *Skippyjon Jones* through a critical lens and discerned the stereotypes that are harmful to Latinx children conveyed through linguistic and cultural caricaturing. Preparing pre-service teachers to be able to discern deficit framing and stereotyping in children's literature may predispose them to choose classroom resources more equitably and responsibly.

Additionally, scholars have found that children's literature is a powerful mode to engage pre-service teachers in difficult conversations (Ivey & Johnston, 2018). To support this, Crawley (2020) examined how exposing pre-service teachers ($n = 42$) to multicultural literature precipitated discussions about two focal topics concerning children's literature, "(1) emphasizing windows and mirrors and (2) considering stakeholder responses" (p.113). To discern specific attitudes pre-service teachers cultivated about children's literature, Crawley outlines two focal strategies, a book analysis of diverse representations in children's literature, including critical topics, such as those of chronic illness and sexual orientation, to convey how certain books can be mirrors for some, while windows for others. In addition to engaging pre-service teachers in discussions about books as windows and mirrors to diverse identities, the pre-service teachers also participated in role-play activities assuming the roles of stakeholders, such as parents, teachers, and administrators by which they experienced greater connectedness with their craft, felt alleviated by practicing talking with "parents" about using diverse books, and explored possibilities for incorporating critical literacy strategies in their future practice. Pre-service teachers recognized the need to include authentic narratives that engage students' cultural and social capital, experiences, and perspectives. Furthermore, Vaughn et al. (2015) found that pre-service teachers were able to negotiate critical topics during a semester-long critical literature unit. During the in-class space, teacher candidates "[listened] to the questions posed, they used each other's questions as a springboard to engage in a discussion exploring social class tensions, cultural ties, and constraints" (p. 29). Similarly, Hoppe (2022), found that pre-service teachers (*n* = 6) majoring in elementary education participated in read alouds featuring the following texts: *A Place Inside of Me: A Poem to Heal the Heart* (Elliott & Denmon, 2020), a picture book about the perceptions and emotions of a young Black man about the Black Lives Matter movement and *We Are Water Protectors,* a picture book inspired by Indigenous movements to protect the earth and its resources (Lindstrom & Goade, 2020). Hoppe (2022) used poetry to facilitate empathy in a teacher-led read aloud to prompt genuine student reactions by way of critically engaging with matters of identity, culture, and global issues and phenomena. Strong factors for reading interest were the acknowledgment of the multiple perspectives, the appeal of the narrative, and the ability to develop empathy and learn about the world through social justice texts, with each of these studies showing how teacher educators can support pre-service teachers' learning to teach from a critical perspective.

The changing global population, increased levels of migration, heightened human disparities in a postpandemic world, the devastating effects of human displacement, and scarcity of resources portray the need for the increase of diversity representation across the globe. Promoting a culture of tolerance, global awareness, and peace education is of great importance along with the necessity to foster a deep understanding of diverse human conditions and the state of the world. For this reason, the increased need for critical literacy for equitable and just practices within systems of education with clear curricular guidelines is necessary now more than ever (Luke, 2018).

Several studies have outlined the importance of critical literacy teaching in teacher preparation as embedded practice in the university curricula (Crawford-Garrett et al., 2020; Riley & Crawford-Garrett, 2022). In DiGiacomo and Gutiérrez (2020), predominately White and middle-class pre-service teachers and elementary school students from nondominant communities took part in an afterschool university-school partnership titled, *El Pueblo Mágico* (the magical community) and engaged with the cultural and historical repertoires of students to enhance their learning of critical pedagogies. While in some instances pre-service teachers defaulted to using traditional didactical approaches (such as when organizing activities that followed traditional teacher-student power dynamics), in others, they engaged in authentic discourse and participated in dynamic and equitable learning structures. This study offers insights into how teacher education can be transformed to focus on teaching as learning of cultural funds, dynamic participation, and critical tools as artifacts for equitable and responsive practices. Similarly, Wessel-Powell and Bentley (2022) highlight how four teachers engaged in critical inquiry through children's literature. Two pre-service teachers specifically chose culturally responsive texts to use when tutoring students of Color, *Tar Beach* (Ringgold, 1991) and *The Bus Ride* (Miller, 1998). Consistent with previous studies on critical literacy in pre-service teacher education, these two pre-service teachers struggled with ways to engage with the layered meanings in the texts, especially in connecting past events with the students' present realities. For example, Nola (a pre-service teacher) had difficulty evoking Rosa Parks's experiences when she boarded a bus in the 1960s in fear that the students might assume that the same could happen to them. Drawing from the data in this study, the authors and teacher educators place focus on reflective practice and cultivating a critical lens in pre-service teachers as an underlying factor in teaching literacy. Moreover, structured critical literacy practices can guide pre-service teachers in their analysis of texts. For instance, Linder and Falk-Ross (2020) used a critical literacy graphic organizer, which prompted pre-service teachers to read children's literature through a critical lens. Pre-service teachers ($n = 97$) participated in a critical literacy methods course where they analyzed children's literature, modeled after an example in class using the text *The Rainbow Fish* (Phister, 1992) and answered questions focusing on interrogating injustices, the sociopolitical context, and messages conveyed in the text with teaching implications for classroom practice. The researchers conceive that pre-service teachers need further support to read beyond the surface of the text and illustrations in picture books. Inquiries about identifying perspectives that are omitted and also identifying the author's message were useful strategies to prompt pre-service teachers to think critically using children's literature and by applying the graphic organizer as a scaffolded guide to critical literacy.

Closely connected to critical literacy is reflective practice, which underscores the importance of self-analysis in teacher education of pre-service teachers' "visions and [...] personal ideologies and histories" (Vaughn & Kuby, 2019, p. 1). For this reason, pre-service teachers cannot learn about pedagogy without acknowledging how their prior experiences with schooling shape their ideas about teaching and also without understanding the population of students they will serve, which is why Briceño and Rodriguez-Mojica (2022) engaged pre-service teachers ($n = 77$) in an activity where they authored picture books guided by critical literacy tenets. Pre-service teachers' writing process was guided by four critical literacy tenets focusing on students' cultural identities, sociopolitical contexts, messages, and text design (Vasquez et al., 2019). This activity was more conducive to facilitating reflective practice and self-analysis than traditional lessons as pre-service teachers created their own literacy artifacts and read them as a group, allowing them to explore different perspectives on critical issues. These studies underscore the necessity for explicit and scaffolded critical literacy practice in teacher education and support how "Critical literacy as a way of being and doing in the world contributes to creating spaces to take on these sorts of issues, engaging learners in powerful and pleasurable ways and creating spaces to achieve a better life for all" (Vasquez et al., 2019, p. 308).

As in these studies and in our work with pre-service teachers, we found that reading critical texts from a critical perspective can challenge master narratives and authoritative sources of knowledge in beginning teachers. Engaging pre-service teachers in critical conversations through literature can help to facilitate multiple perspectives. For example, one illustrative example we found across our research can be seen in the following reflection of a White, European American teacher candidate, Lauren (pseudonym), who was prompted to think deeply about her educational ideology after reading *A Different Mirror: A History of Multicultural America* (Takaki, 1993). Lauren explained how reading this text drew her attention to "the classic White male perspective on history" (Sotirovska & Vaughn, 2022a, p. 14) and helped her realize that she took this perspective as commonplace and never questioned it or looked at history through other lenses. Lauren gained a new understanding of historical events and phenomena, which triggered "an overwhelming aha moment . . . [which she described as] a moment of clarity but also a moment of confusion" (Sotirovska & Vaughn, 2022a, p. 14). As this example suggests, the teacher candidate learned that there are multiple perspectives in what she perceived to be definite, authoritative, and factual knowledge and exemplifies how applying a critical lens changes one's understanding of dominant narratives. Additionally, across our research, we can see that Ana (pseudonym) experienced points of tension, where the literacy artifacts acted as a catalyst to critical literacy learning for this pre-service teacher. In her literacy methods course, Ana was introduced to multiple perspectives of looking at historical events and "realized that growing up, the lessons [she] was taught weren't as well researched as they should have been," and instead, they were often taught from a single perspective and "from one source" (Sotirovska & Vaughn, 2022a, p. 15), and it took additional research in her teacher preparation classes to uncover different perspectives and form a more robust understanding of historical events (see Sotirovska & Vaughn, 2022a, p. 15).

Ana's example underscores the need to embed critical literacy in teacher education as a way to teach the curriculum from multiple perspectives and to reflect on conflicting understandings these perspectives may create in pre-service teachers' practice. Questioning master narratives as a critical literacy skill allows for equity to be the basis of pre-service teacher critical literacy praxis. Inviting discussions about historical tropes through a critical perspective opens spaces for critical practice that extends beyond the traditional models of teaching literacy (i.e., focus on drills, explicit phonics instruction, fluency-first approaches, and others). Jessica's and Lauren's responses warrant such ways to introduce critical literacy supports within their teaching visions of their praxis. Jessica reported that she would feel "a bit uncomfortable when [she will be] teaching about the indentured and enslaved people of America" because she feared that she might "say the wrong thing and accidentally offend some students," while at the same time, she grappled with the possibility of using "a book that the parents feel strongly against" (Sotirovska & Vaughn, 2022a, p. 15). These worries about creating tensions in teaching critical topics and using critical texts to bring attention to sociopolitical phenomena in the class-room truly seeped into Jessica's vision of teaching literacy and left her with many unanswered questions and concerns. Much like Jessica, Lauren echoed similar worries over the selection of children's literature and the potential backlash from other stakeholders in the school, such as parents, caregivers, and guardians with whom pre-service teachers are building a relationship. This relationship between teaching literacy and the larger school community is referenced below in Lauren's response,

> Student choice is important, but it is also important as a classroom commu-nity to read the same thing. It depends on the situation. I would do a whole class read aloud and everyone could participate but have student choice for certain things like a project, personal reading, and all that kind of stuff. It is important to be engaging but if a parent disagrees, "we can't have this," I would have a list of choices – the student can read one of these five books, and then they [the parents] can choose together and talk with their kid. (Sotirovska & Vaughn, 2020)

Like in these illustrative examples of pre-service teachers' grappling with adopting critical literacy practices within their teaching perspectives, teacher educators must also grapple with these findings and create spaces for pre-service teachers to further engage in critical reflective work (Luke, 2018) and targeted coursework is necessary to develop these critical dispositions in teacher candidates. This is why teacher educators should facilitate discussions where pre-service teachers engage in praxis through case studies and scenarios of critical literacy teaching (see Sections 6 and 9) and where teacher educators and pre-service teachers work through these anticipated challenges together to build pre-service teachers' confidence to disrupt the curricular status quo and work toward social justice teaching (Lewison et al., 2002) when they assume classroom positions.

The increasing focus on curricular assessment and meeting state-mandated objectives and standards, curricular programming, and scripted literacy lesson planning leaves little space for teacher educators to implement crucial supports aimed at critical literacy (Sherfinski et al., 2021). Moreover, barriers to successfully implementing critical literacy in teacher education stem from both ideological and practical issues concerning the (mis)understanding of critical literacy as a construct and factor in classroom pedagogy. For instance, Cho (2015) found that pre-service teachers often used critical literacy interchangeably with critical thinking, the latter being a set of skills and strategies for comprehension, while the former encompasses the process of cultivating a social justice lens. The need to implement critical literacy practices becomes necessary in teacher preparation through explicit instruction because, as studies show, pre-service teachers may struggle to cultivate a critical lens on their own. For example, pre-service teachers in both Nganga et al. (2020) and Vaughan (2019) required targeted coursework in the form of a social studies methods course underscored with critical literacy pedagogy and warranted guidance to understanding student success in connection with sociopolitical factors (poverty, racial bias, gender identity discrimination, housing insecurity, and others), rather than solely attributing it to academic dispositions. However, instead of understanding these factors to cultivate a more empathetic lens, Bazemore-Bertrand and Handsfield (2019) and Nayak and Biswal (2020) found that social class and poverty, as influencing factors in literacy, deterred pre-service teachers from apprenticing in schools where socioeconomic challenges persist. Ultimately, Lee (2011) explains that critical literacy and critical thinking may "overlap in certain aspects, [but] the latter should not be reduced to the former" (p. 97) because critical literacy is a practice of analyzing social injustices and the sociopolitical context in which these injustices occur and the power inequities that inadvertently perpetuate them. Therefore, critical literacy is a lens by which phenomena are explored through different viewpoints (Lewison et al., 2002), such as looking at how systemic factors (racial bias, socioeconomic status, gender identity bias, and others) relate to outcomes for individuals and groups in society.

Another barrier to critical literacy learning is the misconception that teaching literacy is a practice that relies solely on disseminating content. To counter this perspective, Hendrix-Soto and Mosley Wetzel (2019), just like Luke (2012) and Janks (2017), remind us that teacher educators need to cultivate critical disposi-tions in pre-service teachers that reflect equitable values and beliefs and evalu-ate their perspectives on critical issues that affect the students they will serve. For example, Anthony-Stevens and Langford (2020) describe how pre-service teachers initially struggled to recognize the value of a course that centered on diversity in rural contexts, which looked at teaching through a geohistorical, sociopolitical, and intersectional lens in a rural pre-service teacher education program. Having courses like this, Anthony-Stevens and Langford (2020) argue, cultivates critical perspectives in pre-service teachers that counter mono-lithic views of rural communities and encourage pre-service teachers to view their own communities as dynamic and diverse. Anthony-Stevens and Langford raise awareness of the Indigenous communities and land-based economies that have shaped the landscapes within which pre-service teachers will teach, which echoes Luke's (2012) views of teaching literacy in congruence with its histor-ical, ideological, and sociopolitical contexts.

Other researchers have found that the enthusiasm to incorporate critical literacy practices dissipates over time as pre-service teachers transition to their practicums (Souto-Manning, 2017). Hence, teacher placement plays an important role in how pre-service teachers view critical literacy teaching and factors into their transition from students learning about theory into their praxis apprenticeships in schools (Freire, 1970; Glass, 2001). Teacher educators thus need to explore these factors with their students and engage in ways to serve their communities after pre-service teachers leave the teacher education class-room. In this section, we summarized critical moments that precipitated the need for critical literacy research in teacher preparation and established the necessity for critical literacy approaches in teacher education. In the following section titled, What is Critical Literacy?, we define critical literacy across the extant literature and contextualize critical literacy practices within the education field. We explore how critical literacy has been documented as a practice, theory, and pedagogy within teacher education and synthesize key models and frameworks, which describe how learners are situated within these systems as well as the affordances that result from them.

3 What Is Critical Literacy?

There are ideological and epistemological tensions in the field of literacy on how beginning teachers should be taught to meet the demands of today's diverse and dynamic classrooms. One perspective emphasizes which skills must be taught to develop knowledgeable literacy teachers. For example, a recent resurgence on the most effective way to teach reading across popular media (i.e., the science of reading, which emphasizes the discrete and explicit teaching of skills) is affecting teacher education programs (Putman & Dixon, 2022). Yet, other perspectives emphasize the essential role of students' and families' funds of knowledge (González et al., 2006) when teaching literacy. Such dynamics highlight the persistent challenges of teaching literacy in teacher education programs. Indeed, teaching literacy is not a neutral skill (Freire, 1970). In addition to these macro policy efforts, teacher candidates continue to experience the apprenticeship of observation phenomenon (Lortie, 2007), which describes that beginning teachers have been apprenticed into understanding school based on their own experiences as students. In that, teacher candidates' teaching may be (mis)informed based on their own observations of teaching as a student.

Moreover, continued research documents that school curricula are relegated to systematic and standardized assessments (Campano et al., 2016) that have failed to support many historically underrepresented students. Teacher candidates, who observe teaching in schools today during their student teaching placements and other learning experiences, may, as a result, see minimal opportunities of exactly what critical literacy looks like in classrooms today (Handsfield, 2018). In our study of pre-service teachers' understandings of critical literacy (Sotirovska & Vaughn, 2022ab), candidates struggled to conceptualize dimensions of critical literacy in teaching practice. Similarly, Giselsson (2020) noted the confusion of what pre-service teachers understood to be critical literacy as the candidates defined it as critical thinking in relation to reading comprehension.

3.1 How Do Scholars Define Critical Literacy?

Critical literacy in education has been oriented toward dismantling inequities, understanding sociopolitical contexts, and enacting actions for social justice (Luke, 2013). Vasquez (2017) defined critical literacy as an epistemic, political, and transgressive stance leading to transformative actions. Described in various ways, critical literacy has been termed as critical consciousness (Freire, 1970), a critical lens (Shor, 1999; Takaki, 1993), a pedagogical framework (Lewison et al., 2002), an emancipatory theory for analysis of power in texts (Bishop, 2014; Botelho & Rudman, 2009; Freire & Macedo, 1987), political discourse and social-epistemic rhetoric (Berlin, 1988) as well as a model for equity, social justice, and advocacy (Janks, 2010; Knoblauch & Brannon, 1993; Vasquez et al., 2019). Although termed in a variety of ways, scholars agree that critical literacy allows for a transformative practice toward equity (Lankshear & McLaren, 1993). What follows are the dimensions of critical literacy outlined in the literature.

3.2 Four Dimensions of Critical Literacy

Critical literacy is a transformative tool for action (Luke, 2013) and enables individuals to examine their roles in the world, engage reflectively with their experiences, and enact change (Blackledge, 2000; Giroux, 1993). Across the literature, critical literacy is conceptualized as a theory rather than a teaching approach and, while it is aimed toward practice, it is actualized as an ideological disposition (Behrman, 2006). Some of the key tenets of critical literacy aimed at classroom practice afford the opportunity to analyze power distributions in society and practice awareness of structures in society that perpetuate inequity (Luke, 2012, 2013, 2018). For example, building from the work of the New London Group (1996, 2000) as a way to disrupt the traditional curriculum to create spaces for expression through redesign, Janks (2010) conceptualized a critical literacy framework aimed at social transformation by unpacking how inequity creates discourses of power and how said discourses can be reconstructed (Janks, 2010, 2013). Janks termed this critical literacy framework the *pedagogy of reconstruction* and included four critical literacy dimensions: power, diversity, access, and design/redesign. Janks argues that transformative reconstruction begins when these critical literacy constructs (power, diversity, access, and design/redesign) are engaged dynamically, informing and influencing each other, to dismantle systems of oppression. Hence, understanding human experience as a product of sociohistorical processes helps individuals engage with these processes through a critical lens (Shor, 1999). In a similar vein, at the core of Lewison et al.'s (2002) critical literacy framework are the understandings of power and diversity as critical constructs in literacy teaching. Lewison et al. stress the importance of reflecting in teachers' practice by interrogating how their actions promote diversity and disrupt power inequities. For this reason, Lewison and colleagues (2002) reviewed twenty years of published literature on critical literacy and deduced four dimensions that operationalize the critical literacy construct. The four dimensions include "disrupting the commonplace, interrogating multiple viewpoints, focusing on sociopolitical issues, and taking action and promoting social justice" (Lewison et al., 2002, p. 382). In the following, we outline each of these four dimensions:

3.2.1 Disrupting the Commonplace

Disrupting the commonplace is a dimension of critical literacy that promotes questioning existing master narratives to examine relationships of power (Lewison et al., 2002). In the classroom, teachers disrupt master narratives by redesigning, questioning, and contesting the standardized curricula. Teacher educators encourage pre-service teachers to juxtapose master narratives with counternarratives to disrupt prevailing dominant discourses in the classroom. With this dimension, teacher educators can encourage pre-service teachers to examine, reorganize, and add to/replace/modify existing curricula.

3.2.2 Interrogating Multiple Viewpoints

Interrogating multiple viewpoints is a dimension of critical literacy that explores dominant and nondominant perspectives, voices heard and silenced, and represented and excluded groups and peoples from spaces of power (Lewison et al., 2002). With this dimension, pre-service teachers widen the curricula to represent plurality, democracy, meritocracy, and equity of funds knowledge, perspectives, and systems beliefs.

3.2.3 Focusing on Sociopolitical Issues

Focusing on sociopolitical issues is a dimension of critical literacy that engages learners to evaluate the sociopolitical system in which we operate, learn, and teach (Lewison et al., 2002). As systems are representations of power, teacher educators encourage pre-service teachers to situate their praxis within systems of power and analyze the sociopolitical relationships that uphold said systems.

3.2.4 Taking Action to Promote Social Justice

Taking action to promote social justice is a dimension of critical literacy that constitutes teaching and learning as acts of social justice (Lewison et al., 2002). As a collective dimension that embodies all the previous dimensions (i.e., disrupting the commonplace, interrogating multiple viewpoints, and focusing on sociopolitical issues), taking action to promote social justice is operational- ized as critical pedagogical praxis where pedagogical theory and activism are embodied through practice. With this dimension, teacher educators encourage pre-service teachers to bridge the classroom (i.e., praxis) with the community and work alongside their students to enact critical literacy for social justice. Each dimension is further broken down into actionable tenets in Table 1.

Scholars have augmented these four dimensions to contextualize critical literacy in practice. For example, Bishop (2014) included an additional tenet to the four dimensions titled, *transformative elements*, which she defines as "reflecting upon actions taken and creating vision(s) for future project(s)" (p. 55). In other words, transformative elements support pre-service teachers' learning aimed at social change in their communities. By adding this tenet to Lewison et al.'s framework, teacher educators can make curricular changes to support pre-service teachers' civic engagement with teaching resources that

Table 1 Critical literacy framework

	Critical literacy dimensions		
Disrupting the commonplace	**Interrogating multiple perspectives**	**Focusing on sociopolitical issues**	**Taking action for social justice**
Adopting a critical stance (Janks, 2013; Lewison et al., 2000, 2002, 2015; Luke, 2018; Vasquez, 2012)	Trying to understand other people's experiences by looking at them from their viewpoints (Lewison et al., 2002; McAllister & Irvine, 2002)	Understanding teaching as a loaded construct (Behrman, 2006; Howard, 2003; Lewison et al., 2002)	Opening spaces for student agency in literacy instruction (Vaughn, Jang, et al., 2020; Vaughn, Premo, et al., 2020)
Looking into the ways knowledge is cultivated (Fitz & Nikolaidis, 2020; Lewison et al., 2000, 2002, 2015)	Analyzing multiple information sources on a particular topic (Guthrie, 2004; Lewison et al., 2002)	Understanding how the instructional context affects learning (Sotirovska & Vaughn, 2022a; White & Cooper, 2015)	Envisioning teaching literacy through reflective practice (Bishop, 2014; Sotirovska & Elhess, 2021; Sotirovska & Vaughn, 2022a)
Examining how texts represent individuals and groups (Janks, 2010; Vasquez, 2012)	Comparing different epistemologies and conceptual views (Luke & Freebody, 1997; Perry, 2012)	Examining disparities in power structures (Lewison et al., 2015; Moje & Lewis, 2007)	Adopting inclusive language to promote equity (Comber, 2001; Van Sluys et al., 2006)

Table 1 (cont.)

Critical literacy dimensions

Disrupting the commonplace	Interrogating multiple perspectives	Focusing on sociopolitical issues	Taking action for social justice
Exploring how classroom literacies construct narratives, peoples, and discourses (Gee, 1990; Vasquez, 2014)	Examining texts (e.g., literacy artifacts, media products, cultural symbols, online materials, etc.) from different perspectives (Johns, 2001; Vaughn & Parsons, 2013)	Examining how discourse shapes power dynamics (Fairclough, 1989; Gee, 1990; Janks, 2010)	Drawing on students' expertise into the curricula (González et al., 2006; Taylor et al., 2008)
Using language as a critical tool to examine power (Botelho & Rudman, 2009; Halliday & Martin, 2003)	Examining how knowledge bases differ (e.g., school knowledge and family knowledge) (González et al., 2006; Lewison et al., 2002)	Situating literacy teaching and learning in a sociopolitical context (Luke, 2018; Nieto, 2015)	Conceptualizing teacher activism as taking action for social justice (Kumashiro, 2015; Lewison et al., 2002; Picower, 2012)
Reimagining teacher roles as mentors, advocates, and learners of pedagogy (Aronowitz & Giroux, 1993; Luke, 2018)	Developing an epistemic stance reflective of open-ended inquiries into the curricula (Lewison et al., 2000; Vaughn & Kuby, 2019)	Understanding how systems of power shape our lived experiences (Gee, 1999; Lewison et al., 2002)	Enacting teaching as praxis for equity (Freire, 1970; Lewison et al., 2000; Reagan & Hambacher, 2021; Sotirovska & Vaughn, 2023)

Note. This table showcases Lewison et al.'s (2002) critical literacy framework with added critical tenets reconceptualized from our recent critical literacy research, including how this framework (Lewison et al., 2002) was actualized in a qualitative study of pre-service teachers' critical literacy beliefs, see Table 1 (Sotirovska & Vaughn, 2022a, p. 5) and in critical literacy survey design, see Table 3 (Sotirovska & Vaughn, 2023, p. 181). Adapted from "Taking on critical literacy: The journey of newcomers and novices," M. Lewison, A. S. Flint, and K. Van Sluys, 2002, *Language Arts, 79*(5), pp. 382–384. Copyright 2002 by the National Council of Teachers of English. Adapted with permission.

underscore local sustainability initiatives (e.g., the United Nations (UN) Book Club (2019) activity that aligns with the UN sustainability framework and the seventeen Sustainable Development Goals, see Section 9.3).

But before pre-service teachers can act in their community for social justice in focused and directed ways, they need to be afforded a space where they can practice critical literacy. As such, George Lee (2020) argues that a prerequisite for critical literacy engagement is a safe environment where learners are not coerced as speakers in the literacy event. While the presence of criteria in interrogating multiple viewpoints, as a dimension of critical literacy, is necessary for evaluating claims and their validity, the need for a safe environment is paramount. One way to accomplish this in teacher preparation programs is through apprenticeships with teacher mentors where pre-service teachers (Crawford-Garrett et al., 2020) practice how to embed objectives that are culturally relevant to students, which also strengthens possibilities for reflective practice and self-analysis (Vasquez et al., 2019). To open safe spaces for criticality, teacher educators must consider the geographies of place when preparing pre-service teachers to enter increasingly diverse classrooms. In developing their critical literacy practice, teacher educators should consider the community's demographics and sociopolitical and geohistorical contexts and bring these contexts into the literacy methods curriculum to highlight underrepresented perspectives, such as those of Black, Indigenous, and People of Color (BIPOC), immigrants, and others whose identities and cultures may not be included in the mainstream curricula. To accomplish this, Han et al. (2020) highlight the importance of scaffolding in the teacher education classroom in preparation for pre-service teachers' engagements in schools with targeted instruction that is responsive to students' identities, geographies of place, and the contexts within which instruction occurs.

Across the literature, we summarize the findings of critical literacy definitions, models, and frameworks (see Table 2), and outline that critical literacy is a pedagogical practice/praxis that actualizes learners' funds of knowledge and agency; it facilitates learners' positionality and citizenry; it transforms learners' identities, and it engages them in civic action and activism for social justice. In this way, " . . . the world is seen as a socially constructed text that can be read" (Vasquez et al., 2019, p. 307). In the following section, we outline a Critical Literacy Pedagogical Practice Framework for cultivating critical literacy practices within teacher education through evaluating knowledge, exploring perspectives, and developing ideology through texts. In addition, we employ the findings from a nationwide research project surveying pre-service teachers about critical literacy and discuss how teacher educators can actualize the Critical Literacy Beliefs Survey (CLBS) items to engage pre-service teachers with critical literacy.

Table 2 Overview of critical literacy models and frameworks

Researcher/ scholar	Components of model/framework	Role of learners	Literacy artifacts	Actions	Outcomes
Freire (1970)	Participatory praxis (practice, apprenticeship, and reflection); Emancipatory theory of empowerment	Teachers learn from students and students from teachers.	Emergence of critical consciousness where reading and writing constitute acts of knowing	Resisting power inequities	Democratic education: to develop critical consciousness to read the word/world
Freebody and Luke (1990)	The four-resource model	Code breaker, text participant, text user, and text analyst	Texts are socially constructed scripts across various technologies and multiliteracies	Critical analysis of texts (engaging schema and ideology)	To read texts with intent, context, and reflexivity
Janks (2000, 2002, 2010, 2013)	Four-dimension framework: power, diversity, access, and design/ redesign. These dimensions entail *access* to power; *domination* as privileged discourses; *diversity* as recognizing cultural and linguistic funds as viable knowledge sources; and *design/redesign* as the multiple modes, media, and multimedia of expression	Creators of new narratives that hold the potential to transcend the current and produce new expressions and works	Analyzing interdependent relationships in texts between and across language, identity, and power	Understanding and dismantling the broader linguistic systems in which dominant discourses operate	To afford possibilities for new constructions of texts as acts of liberation and creativity, resulting in identity and social transformation

Lewison et al. (2002)	Four-dimension framework: disrupting the commonplace, interrogating multiple perspectives, focusing on sociopolitical issues, and taking action to promote social justice	Learners as critical citizens	Texts as constructed artifacts	Positioning texts in cultural contexts to take action for social justice	To take action for social justice
Behrman (2006)	"(1) reading supplementary texts, (2) reading multiple texts, (3) reading from a resistant perspective, (4) producing counter- texts, (5) conducting student-choice research projects, and (6) taking social action" (p. 482)	Text analysts	Student activities and tasks	Questioning dominant narratives and creating counter narratives	Equity
Green and Beavis (2012)	Green's 3D model includes the operational (how to read texts), cultural (how to situate texts), and critical (how to analyze texts).	Learners construct texts	Texts as constructed artifacts	Positioning texts in cultural contexts	To understand how dominant narratives are created
Bishop (2014)	Critical literacy is theorized as activist learning within communities of youth organizing.	Learners as activists	Texts as constructed artifacts	Community action for social justice and change	Youth organizing in out-of-school spaces affords contexts for critical literacy praxis.
Paul (2022)	Critical literacy pedagogy factors comprise, "Relevant, Reflexive, Deconstructive, Dialogic, Empowering, Transformative, and Intersectional" (p. 14).	Learners interrogate ideologies and explore equitable possibilities in the curriculum.	Pedagogical activities	Instructional tasks and activities, including an additional tenet that constitutes a teacher reflection component	These factors describe a critical literacy pedagogy model operationalized as a survey instrument through items that represent instructional and curricular activities for K–12 students.

4 What Does Critical Literacy Look Like in Teacher Education?

The field of critical literacy within teacher education has gained attention across the globe as issues challenging human rights and equity propel educators to address such injustices within their classrooms through decolonizing and empowering pedagogies (Diversi & Moreira, 2016; Ladson-Billings, 2016; Luke, 2018; Sotirovska & Vaughn, 2022a, 2023). Such pedagogies yield transformation and the emergence of critical consciousness in students (Freire, 1970). Teacher education as a situated field in practice aims to prepare beginning teachers to garner pedagogical skills, which they can actualize through praxis. Praxis describes how pedagogical knowledge and practice coalesce through teaching (Freire, 1970). During this process, pre-service teachers take part in various activities – learning theory and methodology of teaching, participating in practicums, performing reflective practice, and growing into their educator roles with aims to serve all students –that transform pre-service teachers' praxis. A goal of this teacher transformation is to develop dispositions toward equitable education practices, which will help beginning teachers and their students dismantle power inequities in their classrooms and the wider social world (Freire, 1970; Janks, 2010; Luke, 2013; Vasquez et al., 2013).

Teacher educators may grapple with the neutrality of teaching literacy as a set of skills and strategies for reading and writing on the one hand and developing ideological orientations in pre-service teachers on the other. The latter perspective challenges the traditional role of teachers as disseminators of knowledge and positions them as *critical citizens* and researchers in the classroom (Morrell, 2015). Additionally, research has pinpointed that pre-service teachers will continue to teach as they were taught unless they are afforded to apprentice with experienced mentor teachers and teacher educators in authentic contexts and teaching scenarios (Lortie, 2007). In fact, a recent study (Sotirovska & Vaughn, 2023) surveying pre-service teachers ($N = 405$) on their critical literacy beliefs in the United States found that the biggest factors contributing to how pre-service teachers learn about teaching were how they were taught in their teaching programs (40.88%) and even more so in their teacher practicums (48.24%), based on participants' answering with agree on a seven-point Likert scale. On the same measure, pre-service teachers reported reservations about the item, *I believe that teaching literacy is a sociopolitical act*, where the highest frequency of pre-service teachers (29.50%) responded with neither agree nor disagree. This result is congruent with findings from other studies where teachers defined teaching as a craft requiring technical skills and subject-area knowledge to be disseminated separately from cultivating ideological stances and dispositions in students, which is key in critical literacy practice

(Cho, 2015; Stallworth et al., 2008). Like these results suggest, in K-12 schools enacting critical literacy is an even more challenging endeavor as research indicates that many in-service teacher mentors are reluctant to address sociopolitical issues in the curriculum fearing parental backlash or simply don't know how to present these issues without coming across as polarizing or controversial (Cho, 2015) and prefer to focus on teaching content and technical skills.

Similar sentiments were expressed by a group of pre-service teachers ($n = 7$) who explored children's literature to address social justice issues in the classroom, where said teachers expressed preferences for anthropomorphic characters conveying universal messages of hope, acceptance, and peace without explicitly delving into politics (Sotirovska & Vaughn, 2022a). However, repeatedly across the literature, the most transformative way to learn about critical literacy pedagogy is through authentic, direct, and ideological investments in discourses where pre-service teachers grapple with their discomfort, question their privileged stance, and examine how said privilege affects their understanding of sociohistorical phenomena (Johnson & Keane, 2023). For instance, pre-service teachers expressed that learning about human atrocities and injustices as statistics was less effective in their understanding of these phenomena than reading personal accounts of historically underrepresented voices (Sotirovska & Vaughn, 2022a). Pre-service teachers reported that learning about personal accounts as lived experiences, rather than subsuming people to statistics, numbers, and graphs, constituted critical moments by which pre-service teachers began developing critical consciousness to read the word/world (Freire, 1970).

Recent research on teacher candidates' preparedness to teach from a critical perspective has established the need for direct and explicit mentorship within a critical framework. For example, Howard (2016) and Nganga et al. (2020) found that beginning teachers lacked practical experiences with critical literacy and struggled to put their pedagogical visions into practice and maintain equitable expectations for historically underrepresented students. In fact, when pre-service teachers expressed their beliefs about student success, they did not consider systemic factors (e.g., racism, poverty, gender identity discrimination, immigration status, etc.) as defining aspects of students' pathways to academic success and focused on students' individual efforts (Vaughan, 2019). In Hendrix-Soto and Mosley Wetzel (2019), pre-service teachers found it challenging to work on incorporating critical literacy in their developing ideologies and such practices were met with tensions and trepidation within their teacher education programs.

In all, findings from across the literature on critical literacy echo the need for teacher educators to support criticality in pre-service teachers' praxis explicitly

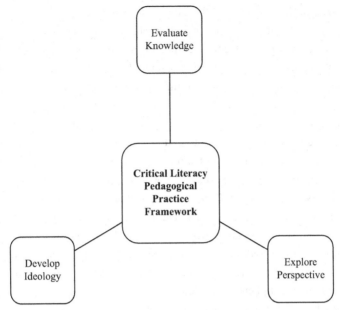

Figure 1 Illustration of the critical literacy pedagogical practice framework

Note. This model features key areas of critical literacy practice for pre-service teachers. Adapted from "Developing a pre-service teachers' critical literacy beliefs instrument" by V. Sotirovska, 2021, University of Idaho ProQuest Dissertations Publishing, p. 18. Copyright 2021 by Vera Sotirovska.

and consistently across the curriculum. As Vasquez et al. (2013) argued, "Curriculum is a metaphor for the lives you want everyone to live and the people you want everyone to be. A literacy curriculum has many goals, two of which are disrupting the commonplace and interrogating multiple perspectives" (p. 51). Vasquez explained that pre-service teachers have to embody said goals first in order to achieve them in practice later. To counter the status quo in teacher education, we, as teacher educators, must find actionable and concrete ways we can engage pre-service teachers' ideologies as they are entering increasingly diverse classrooms. We suggest the following actionable steps to guide teaching for critical literacy in teacher preparation programs (see Figure 1).

This model of critical literacy pedagogical practice includes three transformational aspects of critical literacy, namely ideology, knowledge, and perspective. Within this pedagogical praxis model for critical literacy, pre-service teachers develop ideologies (dominant and counter-dominant), explore perspectives (present and missing), and evaluate knowledge (master narratives and counternarratives). The ideological component denotes the system of beliefs individuals hold, the perspective component denotes how individual systems of beliefs are acted upon, and the knowledge component denotes how individuals form epistemic stances that shape those beliefs.

In the context of critical literacy practice, ideology is defined as a system of beliefs that shape pre-service teachers' political, social, aesthetic, and moral perspectives of the word/world. By developing ideology, pre-service teachers reflect on how their epistemic knowledge is constructed and the sociopolitical circumstances that shaped it (Giroux, 1993). Apart from developing one's ideology, pre-service teachers should also evaluate ideology in connection to power across various learning contexts (e.g., teacher education classroom, practicums, K-12 student experiences, apprenticeships, etc.). For example, Sotirovska & Vaughn (2022a) found that pre-service teachers' ideologies were shaped in interaction with literacy artifacts through praxis with critical picture books, such as *The Proudest Blue: A Story of Hijab and Family* (Muhammad et al., 2019) and nonfiction texts written from nondominant perspectives, such as *Stringing rosaries: The history, the unforgivable, and the healing of Northern Plains American Indian boarding school survivors* (Lajimodiere, 2019) along with critical literacy scaffolding by teacher mentors in structured settings where said mentors and pre-service teachers explored counterhegemonic knowledge sources. These sources hold the possibility to challenge beginning teachers' K-12 beliefs about schooling through counter-narratives that provide differing perspectives on already taught topics through critical artifacts, such as *A Different Mirror: A History of Multicultural America* (Takaki, 1993).

Evaluating knowledge in critical literacy also functions as a lens to assess the relationship between systems of knowledge and power and examine the power dynamics between micro and macro systems, such as those of the text, the school curricula, and educational institutions, and the relationships of discourse that link them. With this component, pre-service teachers can examine their own knowledge, the authoritative knowledge (textbooks), with the knowledge of the students as experts harnessing their worldviews and funds of knowledge into the learning dynamics of the classroom. For example, pre-service teachers can create charts contrasting their knowledge of a topic, that which is presented in their textbook(s), and search for other sources to examine the topic from multiple angles. This may include narrative and fictional accounts of a single phenomenon. For example, pre-service teachers can read literacy artifacts documenting Malala Yousafzai's life and work, an activist for equitable educa-tion for all girls and women, whose narrative has been depicted in various picture books written by herself (Yousafzai, 2017) and others (Frier, 2017; Maslo, 2018), a memoir (Yousafzai, 2013), and a biography (Brown &

Thomson, 2015). Pre-service teachers can engage with Malala's journey as an activist by comparing the narratives and the various media used to engage readers both visually in the picture books and poignantly through Malala's narration in her memoir. Additional knowledge can be gathered by asking pre-service teachers to describe what education activism looks like from their perspectives.

Exploring perspectives is a component of critical literacy by which pre-service teachers examine both emic and etic perspectives, such as those of the stakeholders in the school community, including the children, the parents/caregivers/guardians, the school board, and the perspectives of the outward community by balancing those diverse points of views in practice. For example, engaging with literacy artifacts that produce counternarratives enables pre-service teachers to read texts from contrapuntal perspectives (Said, 2012). Reading fictional and realistic accounts of historical events can communicate incongruent messaging about events in history and as such said texts need to be examined. Implementing targeted instructional practices in the literacy methods courses in teacher preparation is thus instrumental in how teacher educators garner resources that pre-service teachers can actualize in their praxis.

We also suggest that teacher educators implement tools to survey pre-service teachers about critical literacy, such as the Critical Literacy Beliefs Survey (Sotirovska & Vaughn, 2023). This scale was modeled on Lewison et al.'s four critical literacy dimensions and the findings from a qualitative study on pre-service teachers' critical perspectives, after which the model was tested with a sample of pre-service teachers ($N = 405$), resulting in a scale of tenets representing three critical literacy constructs (disrupting the commonplace, focusing on sociopolitical issues, and taking action and promoting social justice) ($n = 11$). By using the CLBS (Critical Literacy Beliefs Survey) scale (see Table 3) in teacher preparation (Sotirovska & Vaughn, 2023), teacher educators can survey their pre-service teachers about their critical literacy beliefs and if pre-service teachers score low on the measure, teacher educators can employ targeted instruction following the Lewison et al.'s adapted framework (see Table 1) for the appropriate dimension. For example, in response to the item from the interrogating multiple perspectives dimension, *I seek out diverse children's literature to share with my students*, teacher educators can support pre-service teachers' knowledge with literacy artifacts (such as picture books) and multimodal media to build a repertoire of resources. For example, teacher educators may include the awarded Orbis Pictus titles from the current year, such as *Nina: A Story of Nina Simone* (Todd & Robinson, 2021), and watch Nina Simone's recorded performances and

Table 3 CLBS content items

CLBS content items
I attempt to understand the sociopolitical systems in which we operate.
I believe my view of teaching literacy is shaped by how I am/was taught at university.
I believe that sociopolitical issues shape my view of teaching literacy.
I believe that teaching literacy is a sociopolitical act.
I believe that teaching literacy is a form of social activism.
I seek out texts to use when teaching literacy where my students can reflect on social justice topics (e.g., racism, class, poverty, gender discrimination, etc.).
I work on developing my view of teaching literacy with social justice in mind.
I seek out diverse children's literature to share with my students.
I take actions in my community to promote social justice.
I am developing lessons with critical literacy in mind.
I try to put my view of social justice into practice.

Note. Reprinted from "Examining pre-service teachers' critical beliefs: Validation of the Critical Literacy Beliefs Survey (CLBS)," by V. Sotirovska and M. Vaughn, 2023, *Teaching Education*, *34*(2), p. 177 (https://doi.org/10.1080/10476210.2022.2049742). Copyright 2022 by Taylor & Francis Ltd. Reprinted by permission of the publisher (Taylor & Francis Ltd, http://www.tandfonline.com).

interviews, and analyze these artifacts against Lewison et al.'s (2002) critical literacy framework. Pre-service teachers can analyze the affordances, barriers, and negotiations that Nina Simone had to navigate to establish herself as a singer and a human rights activist.

With the purpose of transforming their local communities and encouraging literacy initiatives, teacher educators can employ critical literacy practices aimed at sustainability put forth by the United Nations 2030 agenda (United Nations, 2015) directed at young readers. To read across the genres with criticality, the SDG Book Club (2019), guided by the 2030 UN agenda for sustainable development and in alignment with raising awareness toward responsibility and action, included reading lists based on the seventeen sustainable development goals (SDGs) that span themes of poverty, well-being, education, gender equality, climate action, innovation, inequity, sustainability of communities, civic responsibility, peace and systemic justice, and cooperation. Some picture book examples include, *When I Was Eight* (Jordan-Fenton et al., 2013), inspired by the real story of Margaret Olemaun Pokiak-Fenton, an Inuvialuit author and residential school survivor from Canada and *No One Is*

Too Small to Make a Difference (Thunberg, 2019), written by a young activist on climate change, Greta Thunberg.

Coupled with the remaining CLBS tenets, which can serve as a guidepost to gauging pre-service teachers' critical literacy beliefs, teacher educators can incorporate targeted ways to support pre-service teachers' knowledge of diverse literature. For example, referring to the nonprofit organization, We Need Diverse Books (2022), teacher educators can include The Walter Dean Myers awarded and honored titles for younger readers that recognize authors from diverse backgrounds, such as *Red, White, and Whole* (LaRocca, 2021), a picture book about a young Indian American girl coping with her mother's declining health, *Borders* (King & Donovan, 2021), a graphic novel about the barriers Indigenous peoples face focusing strongly on the sense of belonging in a time of strict geographical borders, and *Root Magic* (Royce, 2021), a young adult novel exploring the culture and traditions of the Gullah Geechee people in South Carolina. The way the CLBS tenets can be further actualized in the teacher education classroom is by incorporating literature that supports them. For instance, the interrogating multiple perspectives dimension includes actionable skills, which are crucial in developing literacy potentialities in students. Learning how actively to practice empathy by standing in someone else's shoes, exploring and reflecting on different and conflicting perspectives, analyzing knowledge bases that differ, and developing an epistemic stance through open-ended inquiries are critical ways to connect pre-service teachers with their craft and community. Additional resources for diverse children's literature are featured in the activities section (see Section 9). In the following section, we illustrate how pre-service teachers can leverage critical literacy theory to evaluate classroom literature and engage in critical literacy practices.

5 Engaging Pre-service Teachers in Critical Literacy Practices

Some of the ways teacher educators can engage pre-service teachers in critical literacy praxis constitute (a) performing "deep cultural analyses of textbooks and other instructional materials [and] revis[ing] them for better representations of cultural diversity … " (Gay, 2002, p. 108), (b) performing critical multicultural analysis of texts to consider how "dehumanization, collision, resistance, and agency [. . .] are enacted among characters" and "allow for histories and discourses to bump against each other" (Botelho & Rudman, 2009, p. 269); (c) exercising a critical stance to interrogate inequities that portray diversities through a deficit lens (Souto-Manning, 2017); (d) incorporating counter-narratives by deeply evaluating texts leading to a heightened literacy awareness (McLaughlin & DeVoogd, 2020; Sotirovska & Kelley,

2020; Sotirovska & Vaughn, 2022b; Vaughn, Sotirovska, et al., 2021); and (e) "interrogating and resisting the ideologies" (Campano et al., 2016, p. 33) that associate and disassociate students' academic success with systemic factors (such as race, poverty, gender identity bias, etc.). These actions then must be embodied in pre-service teachers' praxis (Freire, 1970), where theory and practice come together to prepare pre-service teachers for critical literacy work (Lankshear & McClaren, 1993; Lewison et al., 2002).

5.1 Analysis of Texts

Asking questions pertaining to pre-service teachers' beliefs about critical literacy is important to their praxis as they are preparing to take on classroom positions. Narrative approaches to text analysis afford possibilities to shape both "schema and ideology" in pre-service teachers and probing questions can be helpful in facilitating pre-service teachers' ideas about critical literacy. Examples of probing questions are featured in Table 4.

Table 4 Questions for text analysis

Questions for text analysis	How it relates to the critical literacy dimensions
What role does each character play in the narrative? How does each character's action influence the narrative? (Apol, 1998; Apol et al., 2002)	Disrupting the commonplace (Lewison et al., 2002)
Which character(s) are you most interested in learning about? Why? (Vermeule, 2010)	Disrupting the commonplace (Lewison et al., 2002)
Which character stands out to you in the narrative the most? Which character is dynamic, takes action, and evolves throughout the story? (Botelho & Rudman, 2009; Johnson et al., 2017)	Disrupting the commonplace (Lewison et al., 2002)
Which characters are portrayed as more rounded and dynamic (e.g., characters go through changes and experience transformation)? Why do you think these characters are portrayed in this way? (Botelho & Rudman, 2009; Johnson et al., 2017)	Interrogating multiple viewpoints (Lewison et al., 2002)
Which characters are portrayed as more static and one-dimensional? (e.g.,	Interrogating multiple viewpoints (Lewison et al., 2002)

Table 4 (cont.)

Questions for text analysis	How it relates to the critical literacy dimensions
characters do not evolve and may be reduced to one or two characteristics) (Botelho & Rudman, 2009; Johnson et al., 2017)	
How can this story be told differently and whose perspective would you like to hear it from? Why from this perspective? (Apol, 1998; Lewison et al., 2002; Tyson, 2023)	Interrogating multiple viewpoints (Lewison et al., 2002)
How does a retelling of the narrative from the perspective of another character change the outcome of the story? (Apol, 1998; Lewison et al., 2002; Tyson, 2023)	Interrogating multiple viewpoints (Lewison et al., 2002)
How can you relate this story to the real world? How would you go about this? (Botelho & Rudman, 2009; Lewison et al., 2002; Ramsey, 2004)	Focusing on sociopolitical issues (Lewison et al., 2002)
How can you relate this story to students' knowledge funds? How would you go about this? (González et al., 2006; Moll et al., 1992)	Taking action and promoting social justice (Lewison et al., 2002)
How can you relate this story to other stories that provide similar and/or different points of view? How would you go about this? (Johnson et al., 2017; Lewison et al., 2002)	Interrogating multiple viewpoints (Lewison et al., 2002)
Who has the most/least agency in the story? (e.g., who makes choices and decisions that influence other characters and the development of the story?) (Sotirovska & Vaughn, 2022b; Vaughn, Sotirovska, et al., 2021)	Focusing on sociopolitical issues (Lewison et al., 2002)
Who has control over the outcome of the story? In what way does the character(s) exert authority? (Botelho & Rudman, 2009; Johnson et al., 2017)	Focusing on sociopolitical issues (Lewison et al., 2002)
Do you notice any power imbalances in the story? If so, between whom? Why	Focusing on sociopolitical issues (Lewison et al., 2002)

Table 4 (cont.)

Questions for text analysis	How it relates to the critical literacy dimensions
do you think this is? (Bishop, 2014; Botelho & Rudman, 2009)	
What could contribute to more balanced power dynamics among the characters and how would this influence the storyline? (Bishop, 2014; Botelho & Rudman, 2009)	Focusing on sociopolitical issues (Lewison et al., 2002)
Does the book feature diverse characters across race, gender identity, ethnicity, class, ability, etc.? (Botelho & Rudman, 2009; Gay, 2013; Sotirovska & Vaughn, 2022b; Vaughn, Sotirovska, et al., 2021)	Interrogating multiple viewpoints (Lewison et al., 2002)
Does the book feature different representations of sociocultural, geographical, historical contexts, etc.? (Botelho & Rudman, 2009; Gay, 2013; Sotirovska & Vaughn, 2022b)	Interrogating multiple viewpoints (Lewison et al., 2002)
How does the sociocultural context (e.g., the story is set in an underrepresented rural area) portrayed in the book influence the storyline, characters, theme, and conflict in the narrative? (Botelho & Rudman, 2009; Gay, 2013; Vaughn, Sotirovska, et al., 2021)	Focusing on sociopolitical issues (Lewison et al., 2002)
Identify a few quotes and/or images from the book and explore how these quotes/ images can serve as prompts for classroom discussions about social issues (e.g., human rights, equity, climate change, poverty, inclusion, etc.). (Sotirovska, 2021; Vaughn & Kuby, 2019)	
How does the text support critical literacy learning and how can it be reenvisaged as part of the curriculum to meet this criterion? (Janks, 2000; Lewison et al., 2002; Luke, 2000, 2018; Massey et al., 2022)	Taking action and promoting social justice (Lewison et al., 2002)

Table 4 (cont.)

Questions for text analysis	How it relates to the critical literacy dimensions
Does the text hold the potential to act as a springboard for students to take action and promote social justice in their own context? How would you scaffold this activity? (Apol et al., 2002; Johnson & Keane, 2023; Lewison et al., 2002; Vaughn, 2023)	Taking action and promoting social justice (Lewison et al., 2002)

As this table suggests, engaging pre-service teachers with targeted questions about specific texts that portray diverse representations across race, ethnicity, culture, gender identity, and experiences may provide reflective opportunities for pre-service teachers to interrogate their beliefs and make connections to critical literacy tenets. Consider the following examples:

Text 1: *The Me I Choose to Be*

The Me I Choose to Be (Tarpley et al., 2021) is a lyrical poem celebrating children's potentialities through poignant photographs, and it is the winner of the Coretta Scott King/John Steptoe New Talent Illustrator Award. This photo essay can inspire children to be unencumbered in becoming whoever they envision to be by under-scoring the importance of trying, overcoming difficulties, and beginning again. These affirmations can be a springboard for many activities in the classroom and can help children interrogate their visions of their future selves. Featuring diverse perspectives through eighteen long-shot pictures of Black children, these portraits are situated in whimsical settings and are taken against intricate backgrounds. Tarpley et al. (2021) use celestial imagery of planets, stars, and galaxies to showcase the endless possibilities for young children to be as infinite as galaxies and as stellar as planets and stars. Teachers can perform a class read aloud with this book and encourage discussions around student agency, perseverance, and creativity. This book supports student agency activities, such as creating a vision poster of students' interests, dreams, and curiosities. Through positive affirmations, this book also encourages children to persevere through barriers and to keep trying even when they face difficulties. The visual arrangements and props used in the photographs are intentional and aim to captivate every child's imagination by promoting creative expression. Children's books should be windows, mirrors, and sliding glass doors to diverse children's experiences (Bishop, 1990), and children need to see themselves in books; *The Me I Choose to Be* accomplishes that very ideal.

Text 2: *Watercress*

Watercress (Wang & Chin, 2021) is a poignant story about a young Chinese American girl who, by picking watercress off the side of the road with her family, unearths a painful family history. Themes of self-acceptance, sense of belonging, and shame are evoked as the young girl wants to fit in among her peers in Ohio. Throughout the narrative, powerful imagery and language are used to convey subtext and emotion, such as when the protagonist refuses to eat the watercress at the family table in favor of eating store-bought vegetables. The pale watercolor illustrations evoke memories of the great famine in China when the watercress provided sustenance and ensured the survival of the entire family of the protagonist's mother. As the protagonist grapples with her identity, her narration invites multi-perspectivity evoked through a photograph depicting her mother's family. Several pages showcase the protagonist's mother and her family in China in a field of watercress and the painful remembrance of her deceased brother. Apart from interrogating multiple perspectives, this picture book also introduces a point of tension by reconciling the mother's memories of the past with the protagonist's sense of belonging tensed between the two cultures. The protagonist realizes the meaning behind the watercress dish as she associates the familiar and distinct taste of the watercress with her mother's memories of her life in China. Like the protagonist in this story, teachers and students can interrogate their own lived experiences for symbols that bring their families and communities together. Inspired by the new meaning the watercress now holds in the protagonist's life, children can explore their own artifacts and weave personal narratives around them.

Text 3: *Monday's Not Coming*

In *Monday's Not Coming* (Jackson, 2018), the fourteen-year-old protagonist, Claudia, deals with the trauma of the disappearance of Monday, who is her best friend. In this novel, Jackson raises concerns over mental health supports accessibility in underrepresented communities, specifically how schools support children who experience trauma. A central theme in this coming-of-age novel is how the lack of community awareness over Monday's disappearance acted as a pivotal barrier to understanding what happened to her. For example, Claudia engages readers in the disappearance of Monday and brings attention to a critical systemic issue concerning the lack of coverage of the disappearances of Black women and girls in the media and more broadly in society. Claudia's perseverance in finding Monday is actualized through her advocacy and overall acts of agency by which she raises awareness of these critical issues within the school community. Repeatedly, throughout the narrative, to appease her fears about Monday's absence, Claudia relives memories of time spent with her best friend. In this way, Monday's case sparks a discussion over community responsibility and the coping mechanisms young adults who struggle develop as a way to alleviate trauma. *Monday's Not Coming* evokes systemic themes of equity by bringing attention to the importance of representation, a safe space and environment for learning, a sense of belonging, and community awareness.

These three book examples depict historically underrepresented protagonists and highlight issues of visibility and equitable representations of characters in children's and adolescent literature. For example, in *Monday's Not Coming*, Jackson portrays the effects of systemic challenges, perception, media coverage, and vigilance over cases of the disappearance of Black women and girls coupled with the effects of trauma on the mental health development of young adults. In *Monday's Not Coming*, Claudia reconciles her past and present each emerging from a unique set of negotiations (from her struggles as a reader to becoming a student activist raising awareness of Monday's disappearance), allowing the novel to unravel through Claudia's poignant and painful recollections of her friendship. Raising awareness through storytelling is also present in *Watercress* in scenes depicting emotional interactions among family members in which family histories and new traditions are woven together. Further, in *The Me I Choose to Be* (Tarpley et al., 2021), the authors created a platform of visibility to showcase examples of children's agency for society's youngest readers. Coupled with intersectional inclusivity, we also bring attention to the effects of socioeconomic disparities and the lack of systemic supports on mental health in youth through characters in these books whose struggles represent the crux of many adolescent existential plights. However, there is more work to be done to showcase a broader understanding of diversity across race, gender identity, ethnicity, and disabilities so that more children and adolescent readers can see themselves, engage with others and their realities, and experience critical moments leading to a deeper understanding of humanity through literacy.

By highlighting diverse voices in children's literature, educators enhance the potential for books to be mirrors, windows, and sliding glass doors to the world (Bishop, 1990). Ramdarshan and Phillips (2019) contend that today's students are already activists and reading literature with protagonists "from diverse backgrounds and/or featuring inclusive and representative characters is a form of 'imaginary' activism" (p. 6) that holds the potential to change how we conceptualize literacy instruction today. Children's and young adult literature is a unique genre that creates bridges from youth to adolescence and more examples are needed with characters who negotiate barriers and model diverse perspectives, behaviors, and actions, whose imagined realities may be shared with readers. Thus, children's and young adult literature plays an important role in developing critically oriented pre-service teachers and understanding the world in a broader aesthetic, moralistic, and political sense. In the following section, we discuss how critical literacy practices align with adaptive teaching as a pedagogical approach that centers on students' learning needs, knowledge bases, and agency. Moreover, we share a case study to model how teachers can veer away from the planned lesson to leverage students' interests and inquiries and make curricular adaptations by including authentic examples. We illustrate how embedding case studies with real-world classroom examples in teacher education can be a viable tool for teacher educators to familiarize pre-service teachers with adaptive instruction.

6 Adaptive Teaching

Adaptive teaching is an instructional approach that centers on teaching to meet students' instructional, linguistic, and social-emotional needs (Hoffman & Duffy, 2016; Vaughn, 2019). By modifying and adapting instructional actions during the context of a lesson, teachers support the in-the-moment instructional needs of students where students are viewed as knowledgeable meaning-makers. In these contexts, teachers embed practices that are rooted in culturally sustaining and socially just pedagogy (Jackson & Boutte, 2018; Paris, 2012). In other words, adaptive teachers are responsive to students' linguistic repertoires, cultures, and lived histories and backgrounds. Adaptive teaching requires that teachers embed instruction to meet and support students' "cultural knowledge, prior experiences, frames of reference, and performance styles [. . .] to make learning encounters more relevant to and effective for them" (Gay, 2018, p. 36).

To describe the aims of critical literacy, we connect how Luke (2012) expanded on the political meaning behind critical literacy through the "redistributive" and "recognitive" facets of this pedagogy (Fraser, 2009), which aim to allocate resources equitably while also being representative of the diverse funds of experiences, perspectives, and knowledge bases students carry into the curriculum. In that way, Luke (2012) echoes that critical literacy is " . . . a means to broader human agency and individual and collective action – not an end in itself" (p. 6). Luke (2012) expounds that critical literacy in schools engages students in reading through multiple perspectives that warrant intertextual analyses, but he also expresses concerns about whether these practices indeed produce ideological transformations. By focusing on the transformative aspects of critical literacy as pedagogy, Luke operationalized critical literacy skills as tools aimed at transforming political systems and institutions that regulate life and affect how individuals experience the world and themselves in it (Luke, 2013, 2018). For this, educators have to interrogate the resultative effects of critical literacy teaching in systems that are inherently structured around power.

Critical literacy can be utilized by teaching through an adaptive teaching lens. Consider the following example of a first-grade teacher and the ways in which she engages her students in critical conversations about the text. During a read aloud of the story, *The Invisible Boy* (Ludwig, 2013), the boy in the story questions his importance as he feels that those around him and the situations he interacts in make him feel invisible. Throughout the story, the teacher stops and asks students to pair and share with one another any connections about the text and/or ideas springing from the story. One of the students in the class shared that when she is at recess and she tries to play with some of the other kids, she feels invisible at times.

The teacher engages students in a conversation about the idea of feeling invisible. In this particular community, there was an influx of Afghan refugee families. One of the students shared how she wondered if these families feel invisible like the boy in the story. Rather than moving and continuing with the read aloud, the teacher took this student's question and began a more contextualized discussion with students. Why might families from outside of the community feel invisible? How can our community become more inviting to the refugee families and what can we do individually to ensure that others do not feel invisible? What resulted was a week-long unit outlining strategies to help ensure everyone feels seen as well as a school-wide supply drive to support displaced Afghan refugee families in the community.

Such instructional moves where the teacher veered away from her original intended lesson to capitalize on students' ideas and questions signal the powerful role of adaptability during instruction. Moreover, the teacher capitalized on this opportunity to engage her students in critical literacy understandings to start conversations with students about ways to include and counter feelings of invisibility. As this example suggests, modeling to pre-service teachers ways to adapt instruction to support students' queries and to notice and build upon students' questions to elicit and engage in critical conversations is a productive tool to teach critical literacy in teacher preparation programs. Necessary to supporting adaptive teaching are two practices we recommend to ensure that adaptability is centered on critical literacy tenets (see Table 3). Practical strategies to engage in adaptive teaching practices during teacher preparation include critically analyzing literacy curricula and engaging in authentic and relevant practice. These strategies are discussed below.

6.1 Critically Analyzing Literacy Curricula

We encourage pre-service teachers to critically analyze literacy curricula to see the prevalence of critical literacy tenets. This can occur through careful reviewing of the types of texts within the promoted literacy curricula. We encourage candidates to examine who is represented in stories and who is missing (Luke & Freebody, 1997). We also encourage candidates to think about ways to adapt and modify the particular curricular program ranging from modifying text selections to the types of instructional structures put in place to engage students in maximizing opportunities where they have a voice and a sense of agency (Vaughn, Scales, et al., 2021). Janks (2010) suggested that critical literacy is a tool for deconstructing texts to unravel them into their basic composite parts to be reassembled for meaning-making purposes. Such textual reconceptualization and redesign constitute a transformative undertaking. Texts, such as those promoted in literacy curricula, are constructs of power (Luke, 1995) that when analyzed can be reenvisaged and transformed for equity "for enhanced access to mainstream cultural capital requisite for economic and civic participation" (Luke, 2017, p. 12). For example, we see this in many different ways from candidates incorporating authentic high-interest texts that are culturally relevant and connected to students' interests, backgrounds, and ideas (Sotirovska & Vaughn, 2022a) to incorporating broader instructional structures such as the workshop method (Calkins, 1983), where students are involved in the decision-making process of what they read and write.

6.2 Engaging in Authentic and Relevant Practice

To support adaptive and equitable literacy practices that are centered on critical literacy, we encourage pre-service teachers to engage in authentic and relevant practice during their teacher preparation coursework. By modeling to candidates how to structure authentic and culturally sensitive practices that are centered on students' interests and ideas, pre-service teachers can experience firsthand what critically oriented instruction looks like. We see this across the literature in a variety of ways. By developing pre-service teachers' critical consciousness or *conscientization* (Freire, 1970), they can act on oppressive systems and create more equitable avenues of schooling reflective of students' needs.

By placing focus on what individuals can accomplish through critical literacy as a paradigm of social action, adding to the idea of critical literacy as a lens and disposition, Cooper and White (2008) also frame critical literacy as critical self-efficacy by linking the act of reading with the act of questioning narratives to enact social change. In that vein, critical literacy skills materialize in the classroom as self-awareness " . . . with a view to understanding what it means to locate and actively seek out contradictions within modes of life, theories, and substantive intellectual positions" (Bishop, 2014, p. 52) and as an ability to "build access to literate practices and discourse resources" to challenge dominant narratives (Luke, 2000, p. 449). For example, if students have spaces in the curriculum to act on it in order to change it, to invest their own cultural capital into their daily education, and engage in critically reading the community in which they operate and the greater social system within which these practices are enacted, students can transform themselves, their education, and their context of social acting and doing (Bishop, 1990). From this, we can conceive that ideology and power pervade all learning and teaching contexts and these are not neutral activities. In fact, Apple (1992) and Shor and Freire (1987) argued that no pedagogy, curriculum, or act of teaching is neutral. Because teaching is not a neutral act, Bishop (2014) postulates that as teacher educators we must investigate how teaching is carried out in service of democracy and how critical literacy as a pedagogy underscores political directions aimed at equitable teaching practices.

7 Visioning

Visioning is a process by which educators can critically examine their beliefs, passions, and ideals for teaching. It is "a teacher's conscious sense of self, of one's work that rises from deep within the inner teacher and fuels independent thinking" (Duffy, 2002, p. 334). Across our research of visioning over the last decade (Sotirovska & Elhess, 2021; Vaughn & Faircloth, 2011, 2013; Vaughn et al., 2017; Vaughn, 2021; Vaughn, Wall, et al., 2021), like others (Hammerness, 2001, 2003, 2008), we see the vital role of visioning in ensuring equitable practices focused on critically engaged students and teachers. For example, in our early research (Vaughn & Saul, 2013) we examined the role of visioning across ten rural public school teachers and their visions for teaching a variety of subjects across multiple grades ranging from elementary to secondary education. We found that visions centered on three distinct frames, visions of students, teachers, and school. Interestingly, teachers' visions of themselves focused on viewing their roles as "change agents" in their context with the need to ensure they engaged in reflective and leadership practices in their schools to create equitable learning environments for their students. Teachers' reflections about their visions and work in their school included sharing a deep responsibility for working to foster change in their environments to reflect guiding principles of critical thinking and socially just practices. Two of the teachers, Maria and Rachel (pseudonyms) expressed this in their following reflections (Vaughn & Saul, 2013) where Maria stated, "We [teacher leaders] can change what is going on around us," and Rachel added, "I will be the person who opens the door, not the one who waits for it to be opened" (p. 4).

Like these teacher vision reflections show, others from across our research highlight additional aspects of their visions ranging from wanting to create motivated and engaged readers to supporting students who can think for themselves and critically interrogate the world around them. For example,

John, an elementary school teacher, shared his vision as to how teachers can engage students in critical literacy learning, "My vision is that I think they need to learn and to understand . . . Here's a concept, how does it apply to you in your real life, can you use that, or where will you use that in the future?" (Vaughn & Saul, 2013, p. 5).

In this section, we present additional visions of teachers from various content areas that showcase how visioning connects to critical literacy practice. To illustrate, Missy (pseudonym) defined her vision as "having [her] students become informed—like weather, systems and forces in motion—and [. . .] know that social studies isn't just a bunch of dates to remember but they can really relate it to how things are in today's society" (Vaughn, 2013, p. 123). In this way, Missy aims to help students understand society by using the tools she taught them in social studies to become better informed about their present realities. Another teacher, Tammi (pseudonym) focused on leveraging science facts to help students make connections between what they are learning in school and their lives to better understand the world. Tammi explained that her vision is "to make the connections to biology, to physical science, to things that happen in the real world" and facilitate "those connections" through science concepts so that students can "see how it relates to their own lives" (Vaughn, 2013, p. 126).

In another study of teachers' visions in a Native American context, Cynthia (pseudonym) indicated the importance of honoring Indigenous ways of knowing by cultivating student authors that will write about their lived histories as a community. She explains, "As for my vision, I want them to see themselves as writers and their language to be honored and valued, so using their language in their writing" provides a tangible way for students to work toward this goal (Vaughn, 2016, p. 33). With this statement, Cynthia focuses on honoring students' cultural capital and stresses the importance of writing as a medium for authentic representation. This sentiment is also reflected in Yolie's (pseudonym) vision, who encouraged her students to be the storytellers of their communities by authoring books and asked them, "Where are the books written by our people?" (Vaughn, 2016, p. 35). This call to action is strongly felt in Yolie's statement, "My vision is for my kids to be authors—real writers. I just kept those words . . . they just kept coming back to me" (Vaughn, 2016, p. 36). Much like these vision statements and understandings suggest, visioning requires critical reflection of one's beliefs, ideals, and images of what it is we want for students, ourselves, and our school community. Fairbanks and her colleagues (2010) state, "a vision encourages a teacher to look for ways to imbue day-to-day teaching with activity reflective of a unique contribution. It provides a platform from which teachers initiate adaptations" (p. 165).

Adaptability affords a means by which educators can carefully and critically examine their instructional decisions to support students' academic, cultural, and social needs. Moreover, adaptability is deeply connected to critical literacy because it warrants an understanding of students' interests, needs, and knowledge and requires that teachers critically reflect on how students are positioned, the resources used to support students as well as how students' interests, background, prior knowledge, and cultural and language strengths are incorporated into the curriculum. In the following section, we examine how teacher educators can engage pre-service teachers in constructing autoethnographic narratives to interrogate their beliefs about teaching literacy.

8 Autoethnographic Methods for Critical Literacy Praxis

Autoethnography can be a useful method by which pre-service teachers can engage with their experiences as future educators to understand the complex social interactions, the cultural flux, and the dynamics as members of a given community (Hayler, 2012; Pennington, 2007). To engage in autoethnographic work, pre-service teachers must understand the dynamics of a social-cultural system (a system where the cultural and social factors influence one another), learn how culture informs their understanding of the world, and draw on community histories, identities, economies, and environments. Autoethnographic work bounds a group or an individual (or space) (Chang, 2016) and delineates factors that influence members of that group by which they can interrogate their perspectives (Ellis et al., 2011). Hence, teacher educators can leverage Lewison et al.'s (2002) framework to engage pre-service teachers in autoethnographic work to interrogate multiple perspectives, the commonplace, and the sociopolitical context in their critical literacy praxis.

Consider the following example: Pre-service teachers were invited to construct personal narratives in conjunction with the critical literacy theoretical framework (Lewison et al., 2002) taught in a literacy methods course. In this activity, a pre-service teacher, Julia (pseudonym), wrote a personal narrative reflecting on a moment when she found a book to which she can relate. Margaret, who taught the literacy methods course, invited Julia to reflect on past moments, as a child, young adult, or more recent ones when she enjoyed reading a book and to think about how that affected her perspective on children's literature. Julia shared a story about when she read *The Box-Car Children* (Warner, 2010) and how this book made her think about her life experiences and those of others presented in the book. She explained,

> When I read the first *Box-Car Children* book I remember being impacted on a personal level. I think that I read the book in a critical way searching to

understand the perspective and the writing. I found many things that related to my life and many things that did not, which led me to look at the world with a slightly different perspective, for example, homelessness. (Sotirovska & Vaughn, 2020)

As a follow-up, Margaret asked Julia to bring cultural and literacy artifacts that she associates with this critical moment. Julia brought a copy of the book and sticky notes with her comments. She was also encouraged to journal her reactions, responses, and experiences with reading children's and young adult literature, recording the critical moments that marked a deeper understanding as well as moments that created confusion. This autoethnographic activity resulted in Julia envisioning her practice to include critical texts. This excerpt details Julia's reflection,

I will read stories of young students who have made a difference in their school by standing up for what they believe in. There will be many biographies included in these lessons. For example, I would read a biography on Ruby Bridges. (Sotirovska & Vaughn, 2020)

Erin (pseudonym) used autoethnographic methods to interrogate her beliefs about teaching and what resulted from this activity was Erin's vision of teaching for social impact, which extends beyond the classroom. Erin's vision is detailed in the excerpt below,

I greatly believe that students should develop life skills throughout their schooling. I think that this is just one part of that. Throughout life, it will be important for students to be a part of their community and understand and know what is going on in the world.

I hope to do many outside experiences with my students. Some examples would include volunteering for different non-profits, doing a voting simulation, and going to the state capitol building. (Sotirovska & Vaughn, 2020)

In this way, autoethnography served as a method of picking these points of struggle, which in critical literacy theory are referred to as critical moments or socially negotiated experiences, which create transformation (Delgado & Stefancic, 2021). In Julia's case, this critical moment of reading *The Box-Car Children* resulted in a deeper awareness of teaching multiple perspectives and taking action and promoting social justice. Because autoethnography combines a personal narrative approach with sociopolitical contexts (Creswell & Poth, 2016), it allows pre-service teachers to take a stance and engage in open-ended inquiries about their practice to answer questions of pedagogy through a critical lens. Hence, this method also lends itself to pre-service teachers' reflective practice as a way for this group to deeply engage with their craft.

To connect theory to practice through ethnography, pre-service teachers can engage in the following activities: (a) stop and think about how your experiences connect to your practice as a future teacher, (b) identify any critical moments in your learning that created deeper awareness of teaching critically, (c) record assumptions you may have about teaching critically, (d) collect data about your learning of critical literacy that can be cross-examined with critical literacy theory (e.g., examine the critical literacy framework in Table 1), (e) exemplify how you used autoethnography as a method in your inquiry process, and what artifacts you collected as part of this process. With this, we build on prior research to theorize pre-service teachers as developing reflective, agentic, and adaptive educators whose praxis is negotiated by and critically situated in systems of schooling (Clark et al., 2016; Compton-Lilly et al., 2017; Hawkins, 2004).

In summary, pre-service teachers who are prepared to be critically minded educators are likelier (a) to think with students' diverse identities in mind, (b) to include students' cultural funds and those of their communities into the curriculum mindful of geohistorical and sociopolitical contexts, and (c) to act in solidarity with students to understand social issues in their community and the world (Civitillo et al., 2018; Edwards-Groves & Gray, 2008; Vasquez et al., 2019). Pre-service teachers' critical literacy beliefs that are often based on the apprenticeship of observation phenomenon (Lortie, 2007) can be developed through reflective practice to generate possibilities for dismantling systems of oppression to improve students' experiences, academic outcomes, and futures.

Thus far, we summarized seminal research on critical literacy with a focus on Lewison et al.'s critical literacy framework and discussed how the CLBS tenets (see Table 3) can be developed into actionable skills for pre-service teachers using children's and young adult literature examples. Further, we illustrated how adaptive teaching supports critical literacy pedagogy by centering classroom instruction on students' needs, identities, and knowledge bases, where visioning is a key practice by which pre-service teachers can develop critical perspectives and imagine equitable outcomes for students. Finally, we overviewed how pre-service teachers can engage in autoethnographic work as a form of reflective practice to explore future possibilities for critical literacy in the classroom. These approaches and methods hold the potential to strengthen pre-service teachers' critical literacy praxis in ways in which they can enact change and experience transformation to become critical educators (Freire, 1970). Below, we provide additional instructional supports in the form of activities, case studies, prompts, booklists, and other resources for teacher educators to engage pre-service teachers in critical literacy work.

9 Enhancing Critical Literacy Pedagogy in Teacher Education

9.1 Disrupting the Commonplace Dimension

Disrupting the commonplace means re-examining our reality from different angles to gain new understandings of it (Lewison et al., 2002). This dimension addresses how certain norms and standards that we follow are often overlooked and deemed "normal" in everyday life without being evaluated (Lee, 2020). By questioning the commonplace, pre-service teachers can disrupt dominant patterns of thinking about education and open spaces for adaptive instruction. One concrete way to engage teacher candidates in conversations about this dimension is to select mentor texts where candidates can provide alternative pathways toward examining these texts through a new lens. Instead of noting what is commonplace in the text, pre-service teachers can examine: What context(s) is omitted?, what norm(s) is being perpetuated?, what bias(es) is being conveyed?, whose lifestyles, values, and ideas are being promoted? Outlined below, we provide two case studies from across our work about ways such conversations can occur.

9.1.1 Text 1: Skippyjon Jones

As discussed in the opening section of this Element, *Skippyjon Jones* (Schachner, 2007) was the subject of discussion in two undergraduate courses, a literacy methods course and a writing methods course. Since many of the pre-service teachers were in other classes with the authors, in one of the literacy methods classes, we reintroduced the text and invited them to have a conversation about the character portrayals in the story. One pre-service teacher shared that they loved the book, and it was one of their favorites. Another pre-service teacher shared that they also loved hearing how whenever the teachers would read one of the *Skippyjon Jones* books would put on a Spanish accent. During these exchanges, we listened and then began conversations about rethinking the text from another perspective. We asked the pre-service teachers to think about what the text might mean if they were from this culture and spoke the language. How might students who are from Latinx cultures experience the text? Although some pre-service teachers struggled to understand the subtext of the conversation, we continued to ask them targeted questions with the idea of probing, how stories are told, and how we can encourage and facilitate critical conversations to examine the narrative that is being perpetuated in the text. We supported the discussion about this picture book series with three articles (Martínez-Roldán, 2013, 2016; Senta, 2014), which discuss the deficit portrayals in *Skippyjon Jones* for pre-service teachers to gain a deeper understanding of how stereotyping can have deleterious effects on children's perceptions about themselves, their cultures, and the languages they speak.

9.1.2 Text 2: A Fine Dessert: Four Centuries, Four Families, One Delicious Treat

The picture book, *A Fine Dessert* (Jenkins, 2015), documents the preparation of a dessert by four families representing four different generations. In a literacy methods course, Margaret read aloud *A Fine Dessert* with guiding questions to highlight specific scenes. A pre-service teacher said that she first heard about the book in one of her practicum classes when it was used in a mini-lesson by a local elementary school teacher to teach perspectives. Margaret used this opportunity to discuss with the pre-service teachers what is considered commonplace in the picture book. At first glance, the picture book represents four different families across different times in history and captures the preparation of a dessert, with the initial scenes depicting a Black mother and daughter preparing the dessert and serving it to a White family. We asked the pre-service teachers to consider what lifestyles, values, and norms are being promoted in the book. The normalization of "smiling slaves" (Thomas et al., 2016, p. 12) was commonplace in one of the scenes, without narrowing in on the experiences and thought processes of the characters. Hence, pre-service teachers should be asking why the enslaved people are portrayed smiling and eating the leftover dessert in the cupboard and identify the missing context necessary to read the text beyond the culinary thread and family values that are being promoted (Thomas et al., 2016). Margaret pointed out that the book is devoid of a sociohistorical context and presents the asymmetrical power dynamics between the two families. To unpack what is commonplace in this picture book, pre-service teachers must stop and ponder the histories of the groups of people that are omitted, especially when very little context is provided for the characters' actions. In this way, resisting narratives, scenes, or language in picture books to explore what is unsettling or contentious becomes a part of pre-service teachers' critical literacy praxis and can help pre-service teachers recognize texts that may perpetuate harmful and stereotypical depictions of underrepresented groups and omit contexts that are necessary for a more robust understanding of texts.

9.1.3 Activity: Critically Examining Curricula

Examining school curricula through the disrupting the commonplace lens can help teachers determine what and how concepts are being taught and also discern what is missing from the curricula to construct more equitable narratives and espouse diverse viewpoints. Students' funds of knowledge or the cultural beliefs, traditions, narratives, and understandings children bring with them into the classroom are invaluable resources that teachers can weave into the curricula (González et al., 2006). In this way, teachers create opportunities for student identities to be represented in the curricula, which is one way, teachers can disrupt the commonplace and facilitate inclusive schooling experiences. Teacher candidates can analyze the mandated curricula for the grade level and subject area that they would like to teach. Critical activities to align with the disrupting the commonplace dimension can include reflections focused on the following targeted prompts (see Table 5 for these discussion prompts).

Table 5 Guiding questions for literacy curriculum analysis

Examples of probing questions

1. What is missing in the curriculum standards for your grade level?
2. How can you use the critical literacy framework tenets (see Table 3) to increase opportunities for critical literacy?
3. How can you better connect the skills being taught to students' funds of knowledge?
4. What activities do you think students would enjoy that would leverage their funds of knowledge?
5. What textbooks, picture books, and other literacy resources can you add to the curriculum to support students' funds of knowledge?
6. What technological tools can support these activities? (such as videos, collaborative Google Docs, presentation apps, and research websites (e.g., Talk to Books, Google Earth, National Geographic Kids, and others)
7. Analyze the literacy artifacts featured in the curriculum for the grade level texts you are intending to teach and examine (Lewison et al., 2002):
   - How are people and events portrayed?
   - What kind of language is used?
   - Are you noticing bias, complacency, or tropes in the narrative?
   - What is the background context of the narrative?
   - How does this lesson inform/contradict/support your knowledge of the topic it is covering?
   - What other resources cover a similar topic?

In a notebook or a separate document, write down your answers to these prompts and compare how your answers change over time as you add new information.

9.2 Focusing on the Sociopolitical Issues Dimension

Focusing on sociopolitical issues is looking at the context in which we learn (Lewison et al., 2002). Pre-service teachers can leverage their knowledge of this dimension to unpack how systems and structures of power influence students' experiences with schooling. Sociopolitical factors (e.g., racism, gender identity discrimination, poverty, disability discrimination) influence student academic outcomes, wellbeing, and personal development. Fostering critical awareness among pre-service teachers of these factors can better prepare them to teach with equity and social justice in mind.

9.2.1 Activity: What Is the Sociopolitical Context?

Collect various artifacts (picture books, textbooks, young adult novels) on a single topic and examine their sociopolitical context. Three picture books are discussed below, which can be used to model sociopolitical awareness through narratives situated in different geographical contexts.

Text 1: *Emmanuel's Dream: The True Story of Emmanuel Ofosu Yeboah*

This biographical narrative, *Emmanuel's Dream: The True Story of Emmanuel Ofosu Yeboah* (Thompson & Qualls, 2015), is about Emmanuel Ofosu Yeboah and his unrelenting willpower to dispel the stigma around people with disabilities by completing a 400-mile bike ride across Ghana. This text brings awareness to the need for inclusive structures and supports for people of varying abilities to minimize the physical barriers they face. Additionally, this book invites a discussion of how differently abled people are treated in society. Pre-service teachers should be prepared to interrogate the sociopolitical context in the text by inviting discussions on how to create inclusive spaces for people with disabilities and encourage community engagement in creating spaces and infrastructure to support diversity.

Text 2: *Last Stop on Market Street*

Last Stop on Market Street (De la Peña & Robinson, 2017) is about CJ, the protagonist, and his grandma who ride the bus every Sunday after church. While waiting for the bus, CJ begins to wonder why they don't own a car like his friend Colby and instead have to take the bus. CJ looks around at the other children on the bus who have iPads and wonders why he doesn't have one. On the bus, CJ asks his grandma questions about what he observes around him, and his grandma replies with humorous remarks. CJ's grandma points to the perks of taking the bus, such as the diversity of people and experiences, from engaging in conversations about what it means to see with a blind passenger to getting lost in the music of another passenger playing the guitar. Once they get off the bus, CJ laments the dilapidated sidewalks, broken doors, and boarded windows and wonders why the neighborhood is that way. This scene alone can invite robust conversations about varying socioeconomic realities, nondominant communities, urban contexts, and how to engage in action to support the community. Pre-service teachers can interrogate the sociopolitical context in this picture book by opening conversations about socioeconomic inequities and the systemic challenges nondominant communities often face. For example, the last scene in the book showcases CJ and his grandma volunteering at a soup kitchen, an action that aligns with the dimension of taking action and promoting social justice. Pre-service teachers can engage in discussions about how to connect to their communities and suggest ways in which they can take action for social justice in their own contexts.

Text 3: *When Stars Are Scattered*

When Stars Are Scattered (Jamieson et al., 2020) is a graphic novel based on the true-life story of Omar and Hassan who get separated from their mother at a large refugee camp in Dadaab, Kenya after soldiers decimate their village in Somalia. The graphic novel depicts the refugee realities of many displaced people and the trauma, uncertainty, and trepidation they face daily with often inconclusive resolutions. Omar spends fifteen years in the camp under the care of Fatuma as he contemplates ways to help his brother who suffers from seizures. The graphic novel conveys the barriers many refugees face, including the opportunity to pursue education, which is not equitably available to all. The graphic novel portrays six years of Omar's life at the camp after which he is depicted on a plane heading to the United States as part of a resettlement program. Pre-service teachers can engage with the sociopolitical context of the book supported by the resources the authors have shared on their website, including an interview with Omar Mohamed (Mohamed & Jamieson, 2020). The website also features additional resources documenting the perspectives of the people in Dadaab, their resilience, and challenges in pursuit of education, safety, and wellbeing. Teacher educators can leverage these emic perspectives to engage various sociopolitical contexts, which can be aligned with the CLBS tenets (see Table 3) to connect critical literacy theory to practice through guided discussions of these books, read aloud activities, and scaffolded analyses.

9.2.2 Activity: Examine Characters' Agency

Select a picture book or a young adult novel for analysis of the characters' agency. We defined agency as the protagonist's ability to leverage affordances, overcome barriers, and manage negotiations leading to self-actualization, a sense of belonging, and growth (Allen, 2002; Vaughn, Jang, et al., 2020; Vaughn, Sotirovska, et al., 2021). To aid pre-service teachers' analyses of the texts, we defined the following constructs: affordances, barriers, and negotiations. Affordances were defined as the actions, circumstances, and events that supported the character. Barriers were defined as the obstacles, challenges, and problems that impeded the character. Negotiations were defined as the actions the character performed to navigate barriers. Characters' agency becomes visible through the navigation of barriers in the interactions and negotiations with other characters, circumstances, and incidents in the narrative.

To examine characters' agency, write down instances of negotiations noting what resulted for the characters from their interactions in the texts. Examine the individual and collective negotiations characters undertook to navigate barriers and leverage affordances. For example, pre-service teachers can look at the Orbis Pictus award winners and focus on individuals that have showcased agency through their actions by negotiating problems and overcoming difficulties to examine the attributes of these actions (see Vaughn, Sotirovska, et al., 2021).

9.2.3 Activity: Using Critical Literacy Tenets for Lesson Planning

Create a lesson plan focusing on a critical literacy skill based on one of the eleven CLBS tenets (see Table 3) and examine how you would address this tenet and what literacy artifacts (e.g., articles, activities, children's and young adult literature) would support it. Create a reflection notebook or an online document where you write down ideas for a lesson plan.

Below, we provide examples of how the CLBS tenets (Sotirovska & Vaughn, 2023) aligned with the focusing on sociopolitical issues dimension and the way these tenets can be actualized in the teacher education classroom. For example, the following CLBS tenet, *I attempt to understand the sociopolitical systems in which we operate*, can be explored through pre-service teachers' reflecting on how systemic factors shape people's experiences in society using texts, such as *Emmanuel's Dream: The True Story of Emmanuel Ofosu Yeboah* and *Last Stop on Market Street* to increase students' understanding of their community and leverage ideas from texts to make connections between how societal factors shape the way people experience the world and the outcomes that result from those experiences.

Another example of how pre-service teachers can actualize the following CLBS tenet, *I believe my view of teaching literacy is shaped by how I am/was taught at university*, is by reflecting on their own experiences with schooling. Pre-service teachers may recall favorite books they read as K-12 students to explore how this form of reflective thinking can shape their praxis. By selecting a few experiences to ponder through a critical lens, pre-service teachers can begin asking themselves questions about whether they view the text the same way they did as a student, such as how has your experience reading the text changed now vs. then?, what has changed for you in how you perceive the text now and why?, what additional information do you have about the text now that you did not have then?, would you use this text in the classroom?, and if so, how would you use this text with your future students?

9.3 Exploring Multiple Perspectives Dimension

Exploring multiple perspectives means interrogating a social phenomenon through diverse points of view, knowledge bases, and experiences (Lewison et al., 2002). Through this dimension, pre-service teachers examine how exploring nondominant and underrepresented perspectives can deepen their interpretations of texts (Freire, 1970) and facilitate more inclusive understandings of social issues.

9.3.1 Activity: Read the World through Children's Literature

Initiatives calling for inclusive children's literature that showcases people and social phenomena from an equitable perspective include We Need Diverse Books, featuring resources, such as curated booklists of globally recognized children's and young adult literature spanning diverse topics and protagonists, aimed at teaching, learning, and reading. Other resources that offer guidelines for interrogating multiple perspectives through children's literature include SocialJusticeBooks.org (a project of Teaching for Change), an online book depository featuring book reviews and recommendations for teachers, parents, caregivers, and readers with the intention of transforming the world through just and equitable approaches to reading and writing. Other similar initiatives include A Diversity & Cultural Literacy Toolkit, CBC Diversity Committee, Cooperative Children's Book Center, The International Board on Books for Young People (IBBY), and others.

To interrogate multiple perspectives, teacher educators can also familiarize pre-service teachers with the SDG Book Club (2019), an initiative by the United Nations, which aims to bridge children's literature with sustainable development. This book club features reading lists on all seventeen sustainable development goals and includes supporting multimodal artifacts, such as featured videos by the UN Deputy Secretary-General Amina J. Mohammed (Mohammed, 2019) describing the goals of the book club. For example, for Goal 1, No Poverty, which is a sustainable development goal aimed at ending poverty worldwide and ensuring prosperity and wellbeing for all, the UN book club includes four titles, *Serafina's Promise* (Burg, 2013), *Last Stop on Market Street* (De la Peña & Robinson, 2017), *A Chair for My Mother* (Williams & Tuchman, 1982), and *The Happy Prince* (Wilde et al., 1947). Teacher educators can facilitate guided discussions with groups of pre-service teachers to explore different SDGs through children's literature using the critical literacy framework (see Table 1), the CLBS tenets as guides (see Table 3), and the questions for text analysis (see Table 4). To accomplish this, teacher educators can encourage pre-service teachers to join the SDG Book Club and learn about similar initiatives through the SDG Book Club Blog by connecting to other book clubs around the world. The blog emphasizes that each sustainable initiative begins with reading, but the ultimate goal is to take action. The United Nations work closely with the International Publishers Association (IPA), the International Federation of Librarian Associations (IFLA), the European and International Booksellers Federation (EIBA), the International Authors Forum (IAF), and the International Board on Books for Young People (IBBY) to select titles that could facilitate young children's knowledge on the sustainable development goals. Through seventeen reading lists, with each list encompassing a wide array of titles covering at least one of the Sustainable Development Goals, pre-service teachers can begin to develop a praxis at the intersections of critical literacy and sustainable development. For example, pre-service teachers can follow the SDG blog for the newest updates using the hashtags #globalgoals and #SDGBookClub when opportunities for participation in sustainable initiatives arise across various UN global and local platforms and programs, where practitioners around the world share their experiences with implementing the SDG Book Club resources. In this way, pre-service teachers can increase their repertoires of resources and connect theory to practice both locally in their communities and globally by working alongside other international educators for social justice.

9.4 Taking Action and Promoting Social Justice Dimension

To take action and promote social justice means to support all three dimensions of critical literacy (disrupting the commonplace, interrogating multiple viewpoints, and focusing on sociopolitical issues) and enact these dimensions in practice (Lewison et al., 2002). Pre-service teachers can take action by cultivating teaching visions that support the social and emotional wellbeing, funds of knowledge, and identities of students.

9.4.1 Activity: Building Bridges to Promote Social Change

Critically reflect on your vision and take actionable steps in your community to work toward the dimensions of your vision. Consider the following activities:

Idea 1: Engage in reflective work by journalling your praxis. Think about the following prompt: How can you use the four critical literacy dimensions (Lewison et al.., 2002) as a lens to understand your teaching vision? Describe how each dimension (disrupting the commonplace, focusing on sociopolitical issues, interrogating multiple viewpoints, and taking action and promoting social justice) shapes your ideas about teaching. Using Table 1 (table of critical literacy dimensions) as a guide, devise four objectives to work toward in your vision.

Idea 2: Using the eleven CLBS tenets compose a checklist of actionable items toward social change; under each tenet write down steps that you can take to realize this tenet in the context of your teaching. What actions can you take to realize each tenet? For the following CLBS tenet, *I am developing lessons with critical literacy in mind*, pre-service teachers can create activities that honor underrepresented people's funds of knowledge. For instance, pre-service teachers can read *Child of the Flower-Song People* (Amescua & Tonatiuh, 2021), a historical biography about Luz Jiménez, a Nahua girl, who honored her Native culture, language, and traditions through storytelling, with students and facilitate discussions around cultural funds, histories, and artifacts. Teacher educators can incorporate other culturally relevant books from the booklist included in the Appendix section of the Element. For the CLBS tenet, *I believe that sociopolitical issues shape my view of teaching literacy*, pre-service teachers can reflect on how to teach with students' diverse identities in mind. Pre-service teachers can support this tenet by selecting texts that model how individual acts can raise awareness of equity and justice for the entire community, such as *Notable Native People: 50 Indigenous Leaders, Dreamers, and Changemakers from Past and Present* (Keene & Sana, 2021), which addresses Indigenous equity issues through biographical narratives about strength and perseverance. For the CLBS tenet, *I seek out texts to use when teaching literacy where my students can reflect on social justice topics (e.g., racism, class, poverty, gender discrimination, etc.)*, pre-service teachers can incorporate texts that model how characters take actions for social justice. Pre-service teachers can support this tenet by sharing texts with strong examples of agency, such as *I Dissent: Ruth Bader Ginsburg Makes Her Mark* (Levy & Baddeley, 2018), detailing Ginsburg's determination to serve on the US Supreme Court and her dedication to equity and justice for a fair justice system. Coupled with this picture book, pre-service teachers may also examine add-itional sources about Ruth Bader Ginsburg's life and work, including speeches, biographies, and articles detailing her actions toward social justice.

Idea 3: Rural, urban, and suburban geographies constitute diverse and dynamic communities. With your community and your students' diverse identities in mind, create a vision poster picturing yourself as a mentor, advocate, and learner of pedagogy (Aronowitz & Giroux, 1993); how is this vision helping you understand these identities better? What does the role of being a mentor, advo-cate, and teacher-learner look like for you? You may use a variety of materials and mediums to express your teaching vision. How do you plan to make this vision come to fruition; what steps can you take to begin enacting these roles in your local community?

Describe your community and your role in it as a teacher of literacy. How is this vision conducive to adaptive teaching? What does this look like in the context of your own practice?

Brainstorm ideas about how you can be adaptive using Lewison et al.'s (2002) critical literacy framework (see Table 1). As you analyze the critical literacy framework (Lewison et al., 2002), consider the following, which dimension are you most/least comfortable implementing in your teaching practice and why? and how can you implement this framework outside of your teaching and into the community? These are some of the few different ways teacher educators can implement activities supported by critical literacy theory to develop critically oriented teacher candidates.

To further explore each critical literacy dimension through K-8 children's and young adult literature, we put together a booklist featuring recently published award-winning literature that showcases diverse protagonists across various geographical contexts who embody agency, perseverance, and resilience. For each book example, we provide a summary and connect the text to one of the four critical literacy dimensions (disrupting the commonplace, interrogating multiple viewpoints, focusing on sociopolitical issues, and taking action and promoting social justice) (Lewison et al., 2002). Please see the Appendix for the complete booklist of children's and young adult literature examples.

10 Conclusion

Global initiatives to raise awareness of accountability, peace education, and social justice have propelled organizations (see United Nations work) around the world to create frameworks that will address these goals equitably and sustainably. Literacy scholars promote educational reform centering on equitable pedagogies, the advancement of human rights, and initiatives to heighten the public's awareness of inclusive approaches to teaching literacy (Luke, 2018; Short, 2019; Vasquez et al., 2019). Such efforts have created contexts where teacher education programs have become platforms for widespread education reform (Mirra & Garcia, 2021). Due to this, scholars emphasize the need to critically examine the practices, tools, and resources teacher preparation programs use to support critical literacy orientations in pre-service teachers (Sotirovska & Vaughn, 2022a, 2023). Considering the growing diverse student population in US schools and around the world in general, teacher education programs must create possibilities for pre-service teachers to cultivate global, egalitarian, and ethical literacy practices and engage them through apprenticeships and practicums to understand how these practices relate to K-12 students

(Souto-Manning, 2017). After all, critical literacy praxis is a cyclical process with ideological and practical underpinnings envisioned as an embodied practice (Bishop, 2014) by which pre-service teachers learn how to cultivate a critical literacy mindset and discern opportunities for enacting critical literacy in their local contexts.

As critical literacy pedagogy is not a one-size-fits-all approach (Luke, 2000), teacher educators must prepare pre-service teachers to be responsive to the idiosyncrasies, identities, and cultures of students and align these knowledge funds with the curricula. Such acts of care (Vaughn, 2023) support the adaptive approaches we have discussed throughout this Element. Also, teacher educators and pre-service teachers must work together to examine their epistemologies as educators and caregivers and interrogate their own beliefs about literacy teaching against sociopolitical contexts to understand students' unique needs (Simpson et al., 2021; Vasquez et al., 2019). Regarding selections of classroom materials, such as children's and young adult literature and other classroom literacy artifacts, teacher educators must not only curate an inclusive corpus of literature but also be cognizant of what Gultekin and May (2020) and Short (2019) argue is vital, which is the accuracy and authenticity of representation. Classroom materials, thus, must reflect real and accurate representations of people and contexts (Janks, 2017), and these materials should connect to students' funds of knowledge as bridges for learning (González et al., 2006). To do so, teacher educators must scaffold ways for pre-service teachers to plan for and encourage student choice into these selections aimed at their future practice. As a result, when pre-service teachers take up classroom positions, they may be likelier to teach literacy by responding to and including students' social capital, lived experiences, and voices as ways of adapting the curricula to be inclusive of student identities. As Luke (2018) echoes, critical literacy is not an exact and regulated practice, but the emergence of critical consciousness in educators that inspires them to stand with their students in solidarity, see the world through a lens of empathy, and take action for justice.

The next steps for advancing the knowledge on criticality in literacy through our practice and research constitute working at the intersections of adaptive teaching and critical literacy pedagogy by exploring contexts where adaptive teachers incorporate Lewison et al.'s framework (disrupting the commonplace, interrogating multiple viewpoints, focusing on sociopolitical issues, and taking action and promoting social justice), the CLBS instrument (Sotirovska & Vaughn, 2023), and activities to enhance critical literacy pedagogy in teacher education (see Section 9) to capture how these practices transform their classrooms and examine how critical literacy tenets can be enacted in K-12 contexts. To accomplish this, we, as teacher educators, must engage in longitudinal research in critical literacy embodiment at various levels of schooling (university and K-12 contexts) and work alongside teachers to explore ways to transform neoliberal education models to include critical conversations about students' selfhoods, mindsets, and visions about the world and them in it. For this reason, we would like to encourage teacher educators to include these critical literacy tools, activities, and practices in their teacher preparation courses and utilize these instructional supports to cultivate criticality as a pedagogical mindset in pre-service teachers.

We also invite teacher educators to confer with their pre-service teachers using the reflective prompts to encourage journaling (see 9.4.1 Activity: Building Bridges to Promote Social Change) as ways to engage pre-service teachers in critical reflective practices and begin envisioning responsive literacy instruction where student agency and voice are invited into the classroom discourse (see Section 5). Thus, conceptualizing teaching as an ethical craft is an integral part of cultivating a critical literacy lens.

Critical literacy practice will look different for everyone as it is highly dependent on contexts, people, and systems. Because of this, we encourage teacher educators to take up visioning (see Section 7) as a practice with their pre-service teachers in their teacher preparation classrooms to envision literacy instruction that is not superimposed but co-created with empathy, care, and justice in mind. From the extant literature on critical literacy practices, we can conclude that said practices have powerful implications for teacher education, and more action teacher research and longitudinal studies are needed to document efforts and outcomes of how critical literacy is cultivated globally in teacher education classrooms. We hope that this Element serves as both a theoretical and practical guide to enhancing educators' understandings of critical literacy.

Appendix

Booklist of Children's and Young Adult Literature

Title	Author and illustrator	Year	Age	Synopsis	Genre	Awards	Critical literacy dimension
Herizon	Daniel W. Vandever and Corey Begay	2021	Elementary	A young Diné girl travels by means of a magical scarf across land and sea.	Fiction (wordless picture book)	American Indian Youth Literature Award	Disrupting the commonplace
My Two Border Towns	David Bowles and Erika Meza	2021	Elementary	A father and son describe the realities of asylum seekers along the Rio Grande River.	Fiction	Americas Award Tomás Rivera Book Award	Disrupting the commonplace
Kwame Nkrumah Midnight Speech for Independence	Useni Eugene Perkins and Laura Freeman	2021	Elementary	Kwame Nkrumah tells the story of Ghana's independence.	Nonfiction	The Children's Africana Book Awards	Disrupting the commonplace
Fry Bread: A Native American Family Story	Kevin Noble Maillard and Juana Martinez-Neal	2019	Elementary	This story in verse portrays the diversity of Native American families through a shared culinary tradition.	Inspired by Native American traditions	Robert F. Sibert Informational Book Medal American Indian Youth Literature Picture Book Honor Winner	Disrupting the commonplace
We Are Little Feminists: Families	Archaa Shrivastav and Lindsey Blakely	2020	Elementary	This book showcases diverse and inclusive representations of families through poignant photos.	Nonfiction	Stonewall Award Winner American Library Association medal	Disrupting the commonplace
Before the Ever After	Jacqueline Woodson	2020	Middle	This novel in verse depicts the struggles of a former professional athlete.	Fiction (chapter book)	The NAACP Image Award The Coretta Scott King Author Award	Disrupting the commonplace

Title	Author	Year	Level	Description	Genre	Awards	Theme
Child of the Flower-Song People	Gloria Amescua and Duncan Tonatiuh	2021	Elementary	This is a lyrical biography about how Luz Jiménez, a Nahua girl, used art to preserve the culture of the Indigenous Nahua people from Mexico.	Nonfiction	Americas Award Pura Belpré Award Author Honor Book	Interrogating multiple perspectives
Out Into the Big Wide Lake	Paul Harbridge and Josée Bisaillon	2021	Elementary	This book details the experiences of a girl with Down syndrome.	Fiction	Ezra Jack Keats Award	Interrogating multiple perspectives
Shirley Chisholm Dared: The Story of the First Black Woman in Congress	Alicia D. Williams and April Harrison	2021	Elementary	This book is a biography of Shirley Chisholm, the first Black woman elected to Congress.	Nonfiction	Jane Addams Children's Book Award	Interrogating multiple perspectives
Calvin	JR Ford, Vanessa Ford, and Kayla Harren	2021	Elementary	A transgender boy gets ready for the first day of school.	Fiction (inspired by the authors' son)	Lambda Literary Award	Interrogating multiple perspectives
Latinitas: Celebrating 40 Big Dreamers	Juliet Menéndez	2021	Elementary and Middle	This book celebrates influential women from Latin America and the United States.	Nonfiction	Orbis Pictus honor book	Interrogating multiple perspectives

Title	Author and illustrator	Year	Age	Synopsis	Genre	Awards	Critical literacy dimension
New Kid: A Graphic Novel	Jerry Craft	2019	Middle	Jordan is starting at a new school where he is one of the few students of Color.	Semi-autobiographical graphic novel	Newbery Medal Coretta Scott King Author Award Kirkus Prize for Young Readers' Literature	Interrogating multiple perspectives
Watercress	Jason Chin and Andrea Wang	2021	Elementary	A young girl bonds with her parents over a traditional dish of watercress that evokes family memories.	Fiction (inspired by many immigrant children's stories)	Asian/Pacific American Award for Literature Caldecott Medal John Newbery Medal/ Caldecott Medal Winner Newbery Honor Book APALA Award Winner	Focusing on sociopolitical issues
How War Changed Rondo	Romana Romanyshyn and Andriy Lesiv	2021	Elementary	This book poignantly depicts the brutal realities of war.	Fiction (inspired by real-life events of the war in Ukraine)	A Kirkus Best Book of 2021: A Best Picture Book for Starting Conversations A USBBY Outstanding International Book of 2022 A Bank Street College of Education Best Book of 2022	Focusing on sociopolitical issues
BOX: Henry Brown Mails Himself to Freedom	Carole Boston Weatherford and Michele Wood	2020	Elementary and Middle	This illustrated biography portrays Henry Brown's bravery and determination to escape slavery.	Nonfiction	Newbery Honor Book	Focusing on sociopolitical issues

Title	Author	Year	Grade Level	Description	Genre	Award	Focus
Borders	Thomas King and Natasha Donovan	2021	Elementary and Middle	This graphic novel conveys an Indigenous family's story about their challenges crossing borders.	Nonfiction (a graphic novel based on the author's lived experiences)	The Walter Honor Book	Focusing on sociopolitical issues
This Promise of Change: One Girl's Story in the Fight for School Equality	Jo Ann Allen Boyce and Debbie Levy	2019	Elementary and Middle	This book portrays Jo Ann Allen's story who among twelve other students fought against segregation at the Clinton High School in Tennessee.	Nonfiction	Robert F. Sibert Informational Book Honor Winner of the 2019 Boston Globe-Horn Book Award for Nonfiction 2020	Focusing on sociopolitical issues
Born Behind Bars	Padma Venkatraman	2020	Middle	As a result of his mother's wrongful conviction, Kabir spends most of his young life in a prison in India. Kabir is seeking to find his place in the world and support his mother.	Fiction	South Asia Book Award	Focusing on sociopolitical issues
We Are Water Protectors	Michaela Goade and Carole Lindstrom	2020	Elementary	Inspired by Indigenous initiatives, this book is a call to action to protect an invaluable resource, water.	Inspired by the many Indigenous-led movements across North America	Caldecott Medal	Taking action and promoting social justice

Title	Author and illustrator	Year	Age	Synopsis	Genre	Awards	Critical literacy dimension
A Sky-Blue Bench	Bahram Rahman and Peggy Collins	2021	Elementary	A young Afghan girl is determined to build a bench to help support her leg and attend school.	Fiction (inspired by real-life events)	Schneider Family Book Honor	Taking action and promoting social justice
Nicky & Vera: A Quiet Hero of the Holocaust and the Children He Rescued	Peter Sís	2021	Elementary	This book illustrates how Nicholas Winton rescued almost 700 children at the onset of World War II.	Nonfiction	Sydney Taylor Book Honor	Taking action and promoting social justice
A Place to Land: Martin Luther King Jr. and the Speech That Inspired a Nation	Barry Wittenstein and Jerry Pinkney	2019	Elementary	This book describes how Martin Luther King, Jr.'s I Have a Dream speech inspires new generations of human rights activists.	Nonfiction	Orbis Pictus Award for Outstanding Nonfiction for Children	Taking action and promoting social justice
Above the Rim: How Elgin Baylor Changed Basketball	Jen Bryant and Frank Morrison	2020	Elementary	This book recounts Elgin Baylor's legacy as a basketball player but also as an activist for social justice.	Nonfiction	2021 Orbis Pictus Award	Taking action and promoting social justice

Title	Author	Year		Description			
You Should See Me in a Crown	Leah Johnson	2020	Middle	Liz dreams of leaving her small town to attend the prestigious Pennington College. Liz enters to compete in the school's prom for a chance to win a scholarship.	Fiction	A Stonewall Honor Book	Taking action and promoting social justice

References

Allen, A. (2002). Power, subjectivity, and agency: Between Arendt and Foucault. *International Journal of Philosophical Studies, 10*(2), 131–149.

Amescua, G., & Tonatiuh, D. (2021). *Child of the flower-song people.* Abrams Books for Young Readers.

Anthony-Stevens, V., & Langford, S. (2020). "What do you need a course like that for?" Conceptualizing diverse ruralities in rural teacher education. *Journal of Teacher Education, 71*(3), 332–344. https://doi.org/10.1177/0022487119861582.

Apol, L. (1998). "But what does this have to do with kids?": Literary theory and children's literature in the teacher education classroom. *Journal of Children's Literature, 24*(2), 32–46.

Apol, L., Sakuma, A., Reynolds, T. M., & Rop, S. K. (2002). "When can we make paper cranes?": Examining pre-service teachers' resistance to critical readings of historical fiction. *Journal of Literacy Research, 34*(4), 429–464.

Apple, M. (1992). The text and cultural politics. *Educational Researcher, 5,* 4–11.

Aronowitz, S., & Giroux, H. A. (1993). *Education still under siege* (2nd ed.). OISE Press.

Baker, J. (2010). *Mirror.* Candlewick Press.

Banks, L. R. (2010). *The Indian in the cupboard.* Yearling.

Bazemore-Bertrand, S., & Handsfield, L. J. (2019). Show & tell: Elementary teacher candidates' perceptions of teaching in high-poverty schools. *Multicultural Education, 26*(3/4), 27–37.

Behrman, E. H. (2006). Teaching about language, power, and text: A review of classroom practices that support critical literacy. *Journal of Adolescent & Adult Literacy, 49*(6), 490–498.

Berlin, J. (1988). Rhetoric and ideology in the writing class. *College English, 50*(5), 477–494.

Bishop, E. (2014). Critical literacy: Bringing theory to praxis. *Journal of Curriculum Theorizing, 30*(1), 51–63.

Bishop, R. S. (1990). Walk tall in the world: African American literature for today's children. *Journal of Negro Education,* 59(4),556–565.

Blackledge, A. (2000). *Literacy, power and social justice.* Trentham Books.

Botelho, M. J., & Rudman, M. K. (2009). *Critical multicultural analysis of children's literature: Mirrors, windows, and doors.* Routledge.

Bowles, D., & Meza, E. (2021). *My two border towns.* Kokila.

Boyce, J. A. A., & Levy, D. (2019). *This Promise of change: One girl's story in the fight for school equality.* Bloomsbury Children's Books.

Brandt, L., & Vogel., V. (2014). *Maddi's fridge.* Flashlight Press.

Briceño, A., & Rodriguez-Mojica, C. (2022). "It made me see what kind of teacher I want to be:" Critical literacy in a pre-service literacy methods course. *Action in Teacher Education, 44*(4), 290–307.

Brown, D. & Thomson, A. (2015). *Who Is Malala Yousafzai?* Grosset & Dunlap.

Bryant, J. & Morrison, F. (2020). *Above the rim: How Elgin Baylor changed basketball.* Abrams Books for Young Readers.

Burg, A. E. (2013). *Serafina's promise.* Scholastic Inc.

Calkins, L. (1983). *Lessons from a child: On the teaching and learning of writing.* Heinemann Educational Books.

Campagnaro, M., Daly, N., & Short, K. G. (2021). Teaching children's literature in the university: New perspectives and challenges for the future. *Journal of Literary Education,* (4), 1–5.

Campano, G., Ghiso, M. P., LeBlanc, R., & Sánchez, L. (2016). "American hunger": Challenging epistemic injustice through collaborative teacher inquiry. In *Teacher education for high poverty schools* (pp. 33–52). Cham: Springer.

Chang, H. (2016). *Autoethnography as method.* Routledge.

Cho, H. (2015). "I love this approach, but find it difficult to jump in with two feet!" Teachers' perceived challenges of employing critical literacy. *English Language Teaching, 8*(6), 69–79. http://dx.doi.org/10.5539/elt.v8n6p69.

Civitillo, S., Juang, L. P., & Schachner, M. K. (2018). Challenging beliefs about cultural diversity in education: A synthesis and critical review of trainings with pre-service teachers. *Educational Research Review, 24,* 67–83.

Clark, J. S., Brown, J. S., & Jandildinov, M. (2016). Enriching preservice teachers' critical reflection through an international videoconference discussion. *Technology, Pedagogy and Education, 25*(4), 431–450.

Comber, B. (2001). Critical literacy: Power and pleasure with language in the early years. *Australian Journal of Language and Literacy, The, 24*(3), 168–181.

Compton-Lilly, C., Papoi, K., Venegas, P., Hamman, L., & Schwabenbauer, B. (2017). Intersectional identity negotiation: The case of young immigrant children. *Journal of Literacy Research, 49*(1), 115–140.

Cooper, K., & White, R. E. (2008). Critical Literacy for school improvement: An action research project. *Improving Schools, 11*(2), 101–113.

Craft, J. (2019). *New kid: A graphic novel.* Quill Tree Books.

Crawford-Garrett, K., Carbajal, D. R., Short, A., Simpson, K., Meyer, E., & Deck-Stevens, E. (2020). Teaching out loud: Critical literacy, intergenerational professional development, and educational transformation in a teacher inquiry community. *The New Educator, 16*(4), 279–295.

Crawley, S. A. (2020). If I knew then what I do now: Fostering pre-service teachers' capacity to promote expansive and critical conversations with children's literature. *Occasional Paper Series, 2020*(44), 12.

Creswell, J. W., & Poth, C. N. (2016). *Qualitative inquiry and research design: Choosing among five approaches*. Sage.

Dahlen, S. P. (2021). Authenticity. In P. Nel, L. Paul, & N. Christensen (Eds.), *Keywords for children's literature* (Vol. 9, pp. 24–27). New York University Press.

De la Peña, M. & Robinson, C. (2017). *Last stop on Market Street*. Puffin.

Delgado, R., & Stefancic, J. (2021). Discerning critical moments. In *Handbook of critical race theory in education* (pp. 22–31). Routledge.

DiGiacomo, D. K., & Gutiérrez, K. D. (2020). Seven chilis: Making visible the complexities in leveraging cultural repertories of practice in a designed teaching and learning environment. In *The Art and Craft of Literacy Pedagogy* (pp. 41–57). Routledge.

Diversi, M., & Moreira, C. (2016). *Betweener talk: Decolonizing knowledge production, pedagogy, and praxis*. Routledge.

Dr. Seuss. (1937). *And to think that I saw it on Mulberry Street*. Vanguard Press.

Dr. Seuss. (1950). *If I ran the zoo*. Random House Books for Young Readers.

Duffy, G. G. (2002). Visioning and the development of outstanding teachers. *Literacy Research and Instruction, 41*(4), 331–343.

Edwards-Groves, C., & Gray, D. (2008). Developing praxis and reflective practice in pre-service teacher education: Affordances and constraints reported by prospective teachers. In *Enabling praxis* (pp. 85–107). Brill Sense.

Elliott, Z., & Denmon, N. (2020). *A place inside of me: A poem to heal the heart*. Farrar, Straus and Giroux (BYR).

Ellis, C., Adams, T. E., & Bochner, A. P. (2011). Autoethnography: an overview. *Qualitative Sozialforschung/Forum: Qualitative Social Research, 12*(1), 273–290.

Fairbanks, C. M., Duffy, G. G., Faircloth, B. S. et al. (2010). Beyond knowledge: Exploring why some teachers are more thoughtfully adaptive than others. *Journal of Teacher Education, 61*(1–2), 161–171.

Fairclough, N. (1989). *Language and power*. Longman.

Fitz, J. A., & Nikolaidis, A. C. (2020). A democratic critique of scripted curriculum. *Journal of Curriculum Studies, 52*(2), 195–213.

Ford, J. R., Ford, V., & Harren, K. (2021). *Calvin*. G.P. Putnam's Sons Books for Young Readers.

Fraser, N. (2009). *Scales of justice: Reimagining political space in a globalizing world* (Vol. 31). Columbia University Press.

Freebody, P., & Luke, A. (1990). Literacies programs: Debates and demands in cultural context. *Prospect: An Australian journal of TESOL*, *5*(3), 7–16.

Freire, P. (1970). *Pedagogy of the oppressed* (M. B. Ramos, Trans). Continuum.

Freire, P., & Macedo, D. (1987). *Literacy: Reading the word and the world*. Bergin & Garvey.

Frier, R. (2017). *Malala: Activist for girls' education*. Charlesbridge.

Gay, G. (2002). Preparing for culturally responsive teaching. *Journal of Teacher Education*, *53*(2), 106–116.

Gay, G. (2013). Teaching to and through cultural diversity. *Curriculum Inquiry*, *43*(1), 48–70.

Gay, G. (2018). *Culturally responsive teaching: Theory, research, and practice*. Teachers College Press.

Gee, J. P. (1990). *Social linguistics and literacies: Ideology in discourses*. Routledge.

Gee, J. P. (1999). New people in new worlds: Networks, the new capitalism and schools. In B. Cope & M. Kalantizis (Eds.), *Multiliteracies: Literacy learning and the design of social futures* (pp. 43–68). Routledge.

George Lee, C. J. (2020). Two plus four dimensions of critical literacy. *Educational Philosophy and Theory*, *52*(1), 79–87.

Ghiso, M. P., Spencer, T., Ngo, L., & Campano, G. (2013). Critical inquiry into literacy teacher education: Accounting for students. In *literacy teacher educators* (pp. 49–64). Brill Sense.

Giroux, H. (1993). Literacy and the politics of difference. In C. Lankshear & P. L. McLaren (Eds.), *Critical literacy: Politics, praxis, and the postmodern* (pp. 367–378). State University of New York Press.

Giselsson, K. (2020). Critical thinking and critical literacy: Mutually exclusive? *International Journal for the Scholarship of Teaching and Learning*, *14*(1), 5.

Glass, R. D. (2001). On Paulo Freire's philosophy of praxis and the foundations of liberation education. *Educational Researcher*, *30*(2), 15–25. https://doi.org/10.3102/0013189X030002015.

González, N., Moll, L. C., & Amanti, C. (Eds.). (2006). *Funds of knowledge: Theorizing practices in households, communities, and classrooms*. Routledge.

Green, W., & Beavis, C. (2012). *Literacy in 3D: An integrated perspective in theory and practice*. Acer Press.

Guerrettaz, A. M., Zahler, T., Sotirovska, V., & Boyd, A. S. (2022). 'We acted like ELLs': A pedagogy of embodiment in preservice teacher education.

Language Teaching Research, 26(6), 1274–1298. https://doi.org/10.1177/1362168820909980.

Gultekin, M., & May, L. (2020). Children's literature as fun-house mirrors, blind spots, and curtains. *The Reading Teacher, 73*(5), 627–635.

Guthrie, J. T. (2004). Teaching for literacy engagement. *Journal of literacy research, 36*(1), 1–30.

Halliday, M. A. K., & Martin, J. R. (2003). *Writing science: Literacy and discursive power.* Taylor & Francis.

Hammerness, K. (2001). Teachers' visions: The role of personal ideals in school reform. *Journal of educational change, 2*(2), 143–163.

Hammerness, K. (2003). Learning to hope, or hoping to learn? The role of vision in the early professional lives of teachers. *Journal of Teacher Education, 54*(1), 43–56.

Hammerness, K. (2008). "If you don't know where you are going, any path will do": The role of teachers' visions in teachers' career paths. *The New Educator, 4*(1), 1–22.

Han, S., Blank, J., & Berson, I. R. (2020). Revisiting reflective practice in an era of teacher education reform: A self-study of an early childhood teacher education program. *Journal of Early Childhood Teacher Education, 41*(2), 162–182.

Handsfield, L. J. (2018). Continuities of privilege and marginality across space and time: Critical autobiographical narrative in teacher education. In J. E. Justice & F. B. Tenore (Eds.), *Becoming critical teacher educators: Narratives of disruption, possibility, and praxis* (pp. 70–84). Routledge.

Harbridge, P., & Bisaillon, J. (2021). *Out into the big wide lake.* Tundra Books.

Hawkins, M. (2004). Researching English language and literacy development in schools. *Educational Researcher, 33*(3), 14–25.

Hayler, M. (2012). *Autoethnography, self-narrative and teacher education* (Vol. 5). Springer Science & Business Media.

Hendrix-Soto, A., & Mosley Wetzel, M. (2019). A review of critical literacies in preservice teacher education: Pedagogies, shifts, and barriers. *Teaching Education, 30*(2), 200–216.

Hoffman, J. V., & Duffy, G. G. (2016). Does thoughtfully adaptive teaching actually exist? A challenge to teacher educators. *Theory into Practice, 55*(3), 172–179.

Hoppe, K. (2022). Engaging pre-service teachers in interactive social justice-themed read-alouds. *Educational Considerations, 48*(1), 2.

Howard, G. R. (2016). *We can't teach what we don't know: White teachers, multiracial schools.* Teachers College Press. https://doi.org/10.1080/2005615x.2017.1383814.

Howard, T. C. (2003). Culturally relevant pedagogy: Ingredients for critical teacher reflection. *Theory into practice, 42*(3), 195–202.

Ishizuka, K. (2019). The cat is out of the bag: Orientalism, anti-Blackness, and White supremacy in Dr. Seuss's children's books. *Research on Diversity in Youth Literature, 1*(2), 4.

Ivey, G., & Fisher, D. (2006). *Creating literacy-rich schools for adolescents.* ASCD.

Ivey, G., & Johnston, P. (2018). Engaging disturbing books. *Journal of Adolescent & Adult Literacy, 62*(2), 143–150.

Jackson, T. O., & Boutte, G. S. (2018). Exploring culturally relevant/responsive pedagogy as praxis in teacher education. *The New Educator, 14*(2), 87–90.

Jackson, T.D. (2018). *Monday's not coming.* Katherine Tegen Books.

Jamieson, V., Mohamed, O., & Geddy, I. (2020). *When stars are scattered.* Faber & Faber.

Janks, H. (2000). Domination, access, diversity, and design: A synthesis for critical literacy education. *Educational Review, 52*, 175–186.

Janks, H. (2002). Critical literacy: Beyond reason. *The Australian Educational Researcher, 29*(1), 7–26.

Janks, H. (2010). *Literacy and power.* Routledge.

Janks, H. (2017). Pathways to critical literacy: A memoir of history, geography, and chance. In J. Justice & F. B. Tenor (Eds.), *Becoming critical teacher educators* (pp. 101–112). Routledge.

Janks, H. (2013). Critical literacy in teaching and research. *Education Inquiry, 4*(2), 225–242.

Jenkins, E. (2015). *A fine dessert: Four centuries, four families, one delicious treat.* Schwartz & Wade.

Johns, A. M. (2001). *Genre in the classroom: Multiple perspectives.* Routledge.

Johnson, E., & Keane, K. (2023). Challenges and successes of learning to teach critical literacy in elementary classes: The experiences of pre-service teachers. *Teaching and teacher education, 125*, 104037.

Johnson, H., Mathis, J., & Short, K. G. (2017). *Critical content analysis of children's and young adult literature* (p. 28). Routledge.

Johnson, L. (2020). *You should see me in a crown.* Scholastic.

Jordan-Fenton, C., Pokiak-Fenton, M. O., & Grimard, G. (2013). *When I was eight.* Annick Press.

Keene, A., & Sana, C. (2021). *Notable Native People: 50 Indigenous leaders, dreamers, and changemakers from past and present.* Ten Speed Press.

Kelly, L. B., Wakefield, W., Caires-Hurley, J. et al. (2021). What is culturally informed literacy instruction? A review of research in p–5 contexts. *Journal of Literacy Research, 53*(1), 75–99.

Kim, H. Y., & Short, K. G. (2019). A Picturebook as a cultural artifact: The influence of embedded ideologies. In H. Johnson, J. Mathis, & K. Short (Eds.), *Critical Content Analysis of Visual Images in Books for Young People* (pp. 245–264). Routledge.

King, T., & Donovan, N. (2021). *Borders*. Little, Brown Books for Young Readers.

Knoblauch, C. H., & Brannon, L. (1993). *Critical teaching and the idea of literacy*. Heinemann Educational Books.

Kumashiro, K. K. (2015). *Against common sense: Teaching and learning toward social justice*. Routledge.

Ladson-Billings, G. (2016). "# Literate lives matter": Black reading, writing, speaking, and listening in the 21st century. *Literacy Research: Theory, Method, and Practice, 65*(1), 141–151. https://doi.org/10.1177/238133691 6661526.

Lajimodiere, D. K. (2019). *Stringing rosaries: The history, the unforgivable, and the healing of Northern Plains American Indian boarding school survivors*. North Dakota State University Press.

Lankshear, C., & McLaren, P. L. (1993). *Critical literacy: Politics, praxis, and the postmodern*. SUNY Press.

LaRocca, R. (2021). *Red, white, and whole*. Quill Tree Books.

Lee, C. J. (2011). Myths about critical literacy: What teachers need to unlearn. *Journal of Language and literacy education, 7*(1), 95–102.

Lee, C. J. (2020). Making critical literacy accessible to pre-service teachers: Why and how? *Mid-Western Educational Researcher, 32*(4), 369–379.

Levy, D., & Baddeley, E. (2018). *I dissent: Ruth Bader Ginsburg makes her mark*. Simon and Schuster.

Lewison, M., Flint, A. S., & Van Sluys, K. (2002). Taking on critical literacy: The journey of newcomers and novices. *Language arts, 79*(5), 382–392.

Lewison, M., Leland, C., & Harste, C. J. (2015). *Creating critical classrooms: Reading and writing with an edge* (2nd ed.). Routledge.

Lewison, M., Leland, C., & Harste, J. (2000). Not in my classroom! The case for using multiview social issues books with children. *Australian Journal of Language and Literacy, The, 23*(1), 8–20.

Linder, R., & Falk-Ross, F. (2020). Preservice teachers taking a critical stance when examining children's literature. *Literacy Research and Instruction, 59*(4), 298–323.

Lindstrom, C., & Goade, M. (2020). *We are water protectors*. Roaring Brook Press.

Look, L. (2010). *Alvin Ho: Allergic to camping, hiking, and other natural disasters* (Vol. 2). Yearling Books.

Lortie, D. C. (2007). *Schoolteacher: A sociological study; with a new preface* (2nd ed.). University of Chicago Press.

Ludwig, T. (2013). *The invisible boy*. Knopf Books for Young Readers.

Luke, A. (1995). Text and discourse in education: An introduction to critical discourse analysis. *Review of research in education, 21*, 3–48.

Luke, A. (2000). Critical literacy in Australia: A matter of context and standpoint. *Journal of Adolescent & Adult Literacy, 43*(5), 448–461.

Luke, A. (2012). Critical literacy: Foundational notes. *Theory into Practice, 51*(1), 4–11.

Luke, A. (2013). Defining critical literacy. In *Moving critical literacies forward* (pp. 37–49). Routledge.

Luke, A. (2017). No grand narrative in sight: On double consciousness and critical literacy. *Literacy research: Theory, method, and practice, 66*(1), 157–182.

Luke, A. (2018). *Critical literacy, schooling, and social justice: The selected works of Allan Luke*. Routledge.

Luke, A., & Freebody, P. (1997). Shaping the social practices of reading. In S. Muspratt, A. Luke, & P. Freebody (Eds.), *Constructing critical literacies: Teaching and learning textual practice* (pp. 185–224). Hampton Press.

Markus, H., & Nurius, P. (1986). Possible selves. *American Psychologist, 41*(9), 954–969. https://doi.org/10.1037//0003-066X.41.9.954.

Maillard, K. N., & Martinez-Neal, J. (2019). *Fry Bread: A Native American family story*. Roaring Brook Press.

Martínez-Roldán, C. M. (2013). The representation of Latinos and the use of Spanish: A critical content analysis of Skippyjon Jones. *Journal of Children's Literature, 39*(1), 5.

Martínez-Roldán, C. M. (2016). When entertainment trumps social concerns: The commodification of Mexican culture and language in Skippyjon Jones. In H. Johnson, C. Mathis, & K. Short (Eds.), *Critical Content Analysis of Children's and Young Adult Literature: Reframing Perspective* (pp. 61–76). Routledge.

Maslo, L. (2018). *Free as a bird: The story of Malala*. Balzer and Bray.

Massey, D. D., Vaughn, M., & Hiebert, E. (2022). Fostering hope with children's literature. *The Reading Teacher, 75*(5), 575–582.

McAllister, G., & Irvine, J. J. (2002). The role of empathy in teaching culturally diverse students: A qualitative study of teachers' beliefs. *Journal of Teacher Education, 53*(5), 433–443.

McLaughlin, M., & DeVoogd, G. (2020). Critical expressionism: Expanding reader response in critical literacy. *The Reading Teacher, 73*(5), 587–595.

Menéndez, J. (2021). *Latinitas: Celebrating 40 big dreamers*. Henry Holt and Co.

Miller, W. (1998). *The bus ride*. Lee & Low Books.

Mirra, N., & Garcia, A. (2021). In search of the meaning and purpose of 21st-century literacy learning: a critical review of research and practice. *Reading Research Quarterly, 56*(3), 463–496.

Mohamed, O., & Jamieson, V. (2020, April 14). *A Conversation with Omar Mohamed and Victoria Jamieson: A presentation filmed for the virtual book launch*. Politics and Prose; Crowdcast. www.crowdcast.io/e/victoria-jamieso nomar-mohamed-when-stars-are-scattered/register

Mohammed, J. A., (2019, April 1). *Special message from UN Deputy Secretary-General Amina J. Mohammed* [Video]. GlobalGoalsUN. https://vimeo.com/327825743.

Moje, E. B., & Lewis, C. (2007). Examining opportunities to learn literacy: The role of critical sociocultural literacy research. In C. Lewis, P. Enciso, & E. B. Moje (Eds.), *Reframing sociocultural research on literacy* (pp. 15–48). Routledge.

Moll, L. C., Amanti, C., Neff, D., & Gonzalez, N. (1992). Funds of knowledge for teaching: Using a qualitative approach to connect homes and classrooms. *Theory into Practice, 31*(2), 132–141.

Morrell, E. (2015). *Critical literacy and urban youth: Pedagogies of access, dissent, and liberation*. Routledge.

Muhammad, I., Ali, S., & Aly, H. (2019). *The proudest blue: A story of hijab and family*. Little, Brown.

Nayak, A., & Biswal, R. (2020). *Poverty: By chance or by choice: "The hidden forces that shape the poor and the poverty"*. Notion Press.

Nel, P. (2014). Was the cat in the hat Black?: Exploring Dr. Seuss's racial imagination. *Children's Literature, 42*(1), 71–98.

New London Group. (2000). A pedagogy of multiliteracies: Designing social futures. In B. Cope & M. Kalantzis (Eds.), *Multiliteracies: Literacy learning and the design of social futures* (pp. 9–38). Macmillan.

New London Group. (1996). A pedagogy of multiliteracies: Designing social futures. *Harvard Educational Review, 66*(1), 60–93.

Nganga, L., Roberts, A., Kambutu, J., & James, J. (2020). Examining pre-service teachers' preparedness and perceptions about teaching controversial issues in social studies. *Journal of Social Studies Research, 44*(1), 77–90. https://doi.org/10.1016/j.jssr.2019.08.001.

Nieto, S. (2015). *The light in their eyes: Creating multicultural learning communities*. Teachers College Press.

Paris, D. (2012). Culturally sustaining pedagogy: A needed change in stance, terminology, and practice. *Educational Researcher, 41*(3), 93–97.

Paul, C. M. (2022). Competing paradigms: Employing quantitative methods to operationalize and validate a pedagogy of critical literacy. *Reading Research Quarterly, 57*(3), 937–955.

Pennington, J. L. (2007). Silence in the classroom/whispers in the halls: Autoethnography as pedagogy in White pre-service teacher education. *Race Ethnicity and Education, 10*(1), 93–113.

Perkins, U. E., & Freeman, L. (2021). *Kwame Nkrumah midnight speech for independence.* Just Us Books.

Perry, K. H. (2012). What Is literacy?–A critical overview of sociocultural perspectives. *Journal of Language and Literacy Education, 8*(1), 50–71.

Pfister, M. (1992). *The rainbow fish.* Simon and Schuster.

Picower, B. (2012). Teacher activism: Enacting a vision for social justice. *Equity & Excellence in Education, 45*(4), 561–574.

Pratt, M. (2021). 6 Dr. Seuss books won't be published for racist images. *AP NEWS.* https://apnews.com/article/dr-seuss-books-racist-images-d8ed18335c03319d72f443594c174513.

Putman, R. S., & Dixon, K. V. (2022). Beyond knowledge: Helping preservice teachers apply the science of reading research in authentic classroom contexts. In *Handbook of research on reconceptualizing preservice teacher preparation in literacy education* (pp. 285–300). IGI Global.

Rahman, B. & Collins, P. (2021). *A sky-blue bench.* Pajama Press.

Ramdarshan Bold, M., & Phillips, L. (2019). Adolescent identities: The untapped power of YA. *Research on Diversity in Youth Literature, 1*(2), 7.

Ramsey, P. G. (2004). *Teaching and learning in a diverse world: Multicultural education for young children* (vol. 93). Teachers College Press.

Reagan, E. M., & Hambacher, E. (2021). Teacher preparation for social justice: A synthesis of the literature, 1999–2019. *Teaching and Teacher Education, 108*, 103520.

Riley, K., & Crawford-Garrett, K. (2022). Critical, contextualized, content-rich: Revisiting the call for humanizing pedagogies in literacy methods instruction. *English Teaching: Practice & Critique, 21*(2), 156–170.

Ringgold F. (1991). *Tar beach.* Knopf Books for Young Readers.

Rodríguez, N. N., Updegraff, A., & Winters, L. A. (2021). Skippyjon, Spanglish, and stereotypes: Engaging and analyzing authentic Latinx children's literature with preservice teachers. In *Handbook of research on teaching diverse youth literature to pre-service professionals* (pp. 103–123). IGI Global.

Romanyshyn, R. & Lesiv, A. (2021). *How war changed Rondo.* Enchanted Lion Books.

Royce, E. (2021). *Root magic.* Walden Pond Press.

Said, E. W. (1994). *Culture and imperialism*. Vintage.

Said, E. W. (2012). *Culture and imperialism*. Vintage.

Schachner, J. (2007). *Skippyjon Jones and the big bones*. Penguin.

Senta, A. (2014). Juan skippy: A critical detournement of Skippyjon Jones. In *Detournement as pedagogical praxis* (pp. 55–78). Brill Sense.

Sherfinski, M., Hayes, S., Zhang, J., & Jalalifard, M. (2021). Grappling with funds of knowledge in rural Appalachia and beyond: Shifting contexts of pre-service teachers. *Action in Teacher Education, 43*(2), 106–127.

Shor, I. (1987). Educating the educators: A Freirean approach to the crisis in teacher education. In I. Shore (Ed.), *Freire for the classroom: A sourcebook for liberatory teaching* (pp. 7–32). Boynton/Cook.

Shor, I. (1999). What is critical literacy? *Journal of Pedagogy, Pluralism, and Practice, 1*(4), 2–32.

Shor, I., & Freire, P. (1987). *A pedagogy for liberation: Dialogues on transforming education*. Greenwood.

Short, K. G. (2019). The dangers of reading globally. *Bookbird: A Journal of International Children's Literature, 57*(2), 1–11.

Shrivastav, A., & Blakely, L. (2020). *We Are little feminists: Families*. Little Feminist.

Simpson, D. Y., Beatty, A. E., & Ballen, C. J. (2021). Teaching between the lines: Representation in science textbooks. *Trends in Ecology & Evolution, 36*(1), 4–8.

Sís, P. (2021). *Nicky & Vera: A quiet hero of the holocaust and the children he rescued*. Norton Young Readers.

Smulders, S. (2002). "The only good Indian": History, race, and representation in Laura Ingalls Wilder's Little house on the prairie. *Children's Literature Association Quarterly, 27*(4), 191–202.

Sotirovska, V. & Vaughn, M. (2020). [Pre-service teachers' critical literacy beliefs] [Unpublished raw data]. Critical Literacy Project.

Sotirovska, V. (2021). *Developing a pre-service teachers' critical literacy beliefs instrument* (Publication No. 28314957) [Doctoral dissertation, University of Idaho]. ProQuest Dissertations and Theses Global.

Sotirovska, V., & Elhess, M. (2021). Negotiating intersectional identities through visioning. *Peabody Journal of Education, 96*(4), 452–464. https:// doi.org/10.1080/0161956X.2021.1965445.

Sotirovska, V., & Kelley, J. (2020). Anthropomorphic characters in children's literature: Windows, mirrors, or sliding glass doors to embodied immigrant experiences. *The Elementary School Journal, 121*(2), 337–355. https://doi .org/10.1086/711054.

Sotirovska, V., & Vaughn, M. (2022a). Developing preservice teachers' critical literacy praxis in a rural teacher education program. *Reading Horizons: A Journal of Literacy and Language Arts, 61*(2), 2. https://scholarworks.wmich.edu/reading_horizons/vol61/iss2/2.

Sotirovska, V., & Vaughn, M. (2022b). The portrayal of characters with dyslexia in children's picture books. *Early Childhood Education Journal, 50*(5), 731–742. https://doi.org/10.1007/s10643-021-01196-z.

Sotirovska, V., & Vaughn, M. (2023). Examining pre-service teachers' critical beliefs: Validation of the critical literacy beliefs survey (CLBS). *Teaching Education, 34*(2), 170–193. https://doi.org/10.1080/10476210.2022.2049742.

Souto-Manning, M. (2017). Generative text sets: Tools for negotiating critically inclusive early childhood teacher education pedagogical practices. *Journal of Early Childhood Teacher Education, 38*(1), 79–101.

Stallworth, B. J., Gibbons, L., & Fauber, L. (2008). It's not on the list: An exploration of teachers' perspectives on using multicultural literature. *Journal of Adolescent and Adult Literacy, 49*, 478–489. https://doi.org/10.1598/JAAL.49.6.3.

Takaki, R. (1993). *A different mirror: A history of multicultural America*. Little, Brown.

Tarpley, N. A., Bethencourt, R., & Bethencourt, K. (2021). *The me I choose to be*. Little, Brown Books for Young Readers.

Taylor, L. K., Bernhard, J. K., Garg, S., & Cummins, J. (2008). Affirming plural belonging: Building on students' family-based cultural and linguistic capital through multiliteracies pedagogy. *Journal of Early Childhood Literacy, 8*(3), 269–294.

Thomas, E. E., Reese, D., & Horning, K. T. (2016). Much ado about a fine dessert: The cultural politics of representing slavery in children's literature. *Journal of Children's Literature, 42*(2), 6–17.

Thompson, L. A., & Qualls, S. (2015). *Emmanuel's dream: The true story of Emmanuel Ofosu*. Schwartz & Wade.

Thunberg, G. (2019). *No one is too small to make a difference*. Penguin.

Todd, T. N., & Robinson, C. (2021). *Nina: A story of Nina Simone*. Penguin.

Tyson, L. (2023). *Critical theory today: A user-friendly guide*. Taylor & Francis.

United Nations. (2015). *Transforming our world: The 2030 agenda for sustainable development*. https://sdgs.un.org/2030agenda.

United Nations. (2019, April). SDG Book Club Blog. www.un.org/sustainabledevelopment/sdgbookclub/blog/.

United Nations. (2019, April). SDG Book Club. www.un.org/sustainabledevelopment/sdgbookclub/.

Van Sluys, K., Lewison, M., & Flint, A. S. (2006). Researching critical literacy: A critical study of analysis of classroom discourse. *Journal of Literacy Research, 38*(2), 197–233.

Vandever, D. W., & Begay, C. (2021). *Herizon*. South of Sunrise Creative.

Vasquez, V. M. (2014). *Negotiating critical literacies with young children*. Routledge.

Vasquez, V. (2012). Critical literacy. In J. Banks (Ed.), *Oxford research encyclopedia of education* (pp. 466–469). Sage. https://doi.org/10.1093/acrefore/9780190264093.013.20.

Vasquez, V. M., Janks, H., & Comber, B. (2019). Critical literacy as a way of being and doing. *Language Arts, 96*(5), 300–311.

Vasquez, V. M., Tate, S. L., & Harste, J. C. (2013). *Negotiating critical literacies with teachers: Theoretical foundations and pedagogical resources for pre-service and in-service contexts*. Routledge.

Vaughn, M. (2015). Adaptive teaching: Reflective practice of two elementary teachers' visions and adaptations during literacy instruction. *Reflective Practice, 16*(1), 43–60.

Vaughan, W. E. (2019). Preparing culturally responsive educators in the 21st century: White pre-service teachers identification of unearned privileges. *Georgia Educational Researcher, 16* (2), Article 2. https://doi.org/10.20429/ger.2019.160204.

Vaughn, M. (2013). Examining teacher agency: Why did Les leave the building? *The New Educator, 9*(2), 119–134.

Vaughn, M. (2016). Re-envisioning literacy in a teacher inquiry group in a Native American context. *Literacy Research and Instruction, 55*(1), 24–47.

Vaughn, M. (2019). Adaptive teaching during reading instruction: A multi-case study. *Reading Psychology, 40*(1), 1–33.

Vaughn, M. (2021). The role of visioning in supporting equitable spaces. *Peabody Journal of Education, 96*(4), 483–490.

Vaughn, M. (2023). Exploring an ethic of care as a way to enhance agency in early childhood. *Early Childhood Education Journal*, 1–9.

Vaughn, M., & Faircloth, B. (2013). Teaching with a purpose in mind: Cultivating a vision. *Professional Educator, 37*(2), 1–12.

Vaughn, M., & Faircloth, B. S. (2011). Understanding teacher visioning and agency during literacy instruction. *60th Yearbook of the Literacy Research Association*, 156–164.

Vaughn, M., & Kuby, C. R. (2019). Fostering critical, relational visionaries: Autoethnographic practices in teacher preparation. *Action in Teacher Education, 41*(2), 117–136.

Vaughn, M., & Parsons, S. A. (2013). Adaptive teachers as innovators: Instructional adaptations opening spaces for enhanced literacy learning. *Language Arts, 91*(2), 81–93.

Vaughn, M., & Saul, M. (2013). Navigating the rural terrain: Educators' visions to promote change. *Rural Educator, 34*(2), n2. https://doi.org/10.35608/rur aled.v34i2.401.

Vaughn, M., Allen, S., Kologi, S., & McGowan, S. (2015). Revisiting literature circles as open spaces for critical discussions. *Journal of Reading Education, 40*(2), 27–32.

Vaughn, M., Jang, B. G., Sotirovska, V., & Cooper-Novack, G. (2020). Student agency in literacy: A systematic review of the literature. *Reading Psychology, 41*(7), 712–734. https://doi.org/10.1080/02702711.2020.1783142.

Vaughn, M., Parsons, S. A., Scales, R. Q., & Wall, A. (2017). Envisioning our practice: Examining and interpreting pedagogical visions of four early career teacher educators. *The New Educator, 13*(3), 251–270.

Vaughn, M., Premo, J., Sotirovska, V. V., & Erickson, D. (2020). Evaluating agency in literacy using the student agency profile. *The Reading Teacher, 73*(4), 427–441. https://doi.org/10.1002/trtr.1853.

Vaughn, M., Scales, R. Q., Stevens, E. Y. et al. (2021). Understanding literacy adoption policies across contexts: A multi-state examination of literacy curriculum decision-making. *Journal of Curriculum Studies, 53*(3), 333–352.

Vaughn, M., Sotirovska, V., Darragh, J. J., & Elhess, M. (2021). Examining agency in children's nonfiction picture books. *Children's Literature in Education,* 1–19. https://doi.org/10.1007/s10583-021-09435-y.

Vaughn, M., Wall, A., Scales, R. Q., Parsons, S. A., & Sotirovska, V. (2021). Teacher visioning: A systematic review of the literature. *Teaching and Teacher Education, 108,* 103502. https://doi.org/10.1016/j.tate.2021.103502.

Venkatraman, P. (2020). *Born behind bars.* Nancy Paulsen Books.

Vermeule, B. (2010). *Why do we care about literary characters?.* JHU Press.

Wang, A. & Chin, J. (2021). *Watercress.* Neal Porter Books.

Warner, G. C. (2010). *The Boxcar children bookshelf (Books# 1-12).* Albert Whitman.

We Need Diverse Books (WNDB). (2022). *Where to Find Diverse Books.* https://diversebooks.org/resources-old/where-to-find-diverse-books/.

Weatherford, C. B., & Wood, M. (2020). *BOX: Henry Brown mails himself to freedom.* Candlewick Press.

Wessel-Powell, C., & Bentley, H. (2022). Newcomers, novices, censors, and seasoned advocates navigate risky texts with critical literacy. *The New Educator, 18*(1–2), 61–86.

White, R. E., & Cooper, K. (2015). *Democracy and its discontents: Critical literacy across global contexts*. Brill.

Wilde, O., Welles, A. B. O., & Herrmann, M. S. B. (1947). *The happy prince*. Decca.

Wilder, L. I. (1935). *Little house in the big woods: Little house on the prairie*. Harper & Row.

Williams, A. D., & Harrison, A. (2021). *Shirley Chisholm dared: The story of the first Black woman in congress*. Anne Schwartz Books.

Williams, V. B., & Tuchman, L. (1982). *A chair for my mother* (p. 32). Greenwillow Books.

Wittenstein, B., & Pinkney, J. (2019). *A place to land: Martin Luther King Jr. and the speech that inspired a nation*. Neal Porter Books.

Woodson, J. (2002). *Visiting day*. Puffin Books.

Yousafzai, M. (2013). *I am Malala: The girl who stood up for education and was shot by the Taliban*. Hachette.

Yousafzai, M. (2017). *Malala's magic pencil*. Little, Brown Books for Young Readers.

Cambridge Elements ≡

Critical Issues in Teacher Education

Tony Loughland
University of New South Wales

Tony Loughland is an Associate Professor in the School of Education at the University of New South Wales, Australia. Tony is currently leading projects on using AI for citizens' informed participation in urban development, the provision of staffing for rural and remote areas in NSW and on Graduate Ready Schools.

Andy Gao
University of New South Wales

Andy Gao is a Professor in the School of Education at the University of New South Wales, Australia. He edits various internationally-renowned journals, such as International Review of Applied Linguistics in Language Teaching for De Gruyter and Asia Pacific Education Researcher for Springer.

Hoa T. M. Nguyen
University of New South Wales

Hoa T. M. Nguyen is an Associate Professor in the School of Education at the University of New South Wales, Australia. She specializes in teacher education/development, mentoring and sociocultural theory.

About the Series
This series addresses the critical issues teacher educators and teachers are engaged with in the increasingly complex profession of teaching. These issues reside in teachers' response to broader social, cultural and political shifts and the need for teachers' professional education to equip them to teach culturally and linguistically diverse students.

Cambridge Elements $\equiv$

Critical Issues in Teacher Education

Elements in the Series

Interculturality, Criticality and Reflexivity in Teacher Education
Fred Dervin

Enhancing Educators' Theoretical and Practical Understandings of Critical Literacy
Vera Sotirovska and Margaret Vaughn

A full series listing is available at: www.cambridge.org/EITE.

Printed in the United States
by Baker & Taylor Publisher Services